Hopetimism

A Case for Biblical Hope

Dedicated To
My God, who deserves all the glory
My Wife, who loves me so beautifully
My Father, who taught me to seek the Lord

Special Thanks To
Judy (Mamaw) McBee, who was the first person to read this book
all the way through. Without her this book would have many
grammatical errors, sentences that go nowhere, and an author
whose life would have been far less blessed without her.

DJ Coleman, who gave me the encouragement and opportunity to
preach and write what now makes up this book. Without his help,
insights, and trademark frankness I'm not sure how many more
years this book would have remained simple study notes in a spiral
bound notebook.

Table of Contents

Foreword By DJ Coleman

There is probably no one else I enjoy having theological conversations with more than Caleb McBee. Caleb has theological depth, Biblical wisdom, timely advice, all from a heart full of love. It was for this reason I was excited for him to write the book you are now holding.

This book will help you to better understand God, yourself, the world, and how this God is calling you to participate in this world.

So often we are conformed to the ways of this world (Rom. 12:2). The world teaches us to be self-absorbed thinking only of ourselves. When this happens, the goal becomes to be optimistic rather than pessimistic. However, Jesus desires for us to have abundant life not an absorbed life. An abundant life comes from the hope held out in the gospel (Col. 1:23). The gospel does not leave us optimistic; the gospel gives us hope.

Optimism is based on possibilities, while hope is based on promises.

Optimism can often leave us frustrated when the outcome does not go the way we wanted. Hope does not disappoint us (Rom. 5:5). This is because hope has to do with the finished work of the cross (John 19:30). I strongly believe a lot of the frustration that many Christians have felt over the last five years has been largely due to an optimistic outlook on life rather than a "hopetimistic" life.

Whether it be political polarization, social unrest, Covid crisis and it's impact or several other realities that have plagued the world.

Christians have suffered just as people who have no hope (1 Thess. 4:13).

God does not want his people to suffer in this way. It is for that reason He has given us the fivefold ministry (Eph. 4:11).

As you read this book you will learn, grow, and mature into a person of faith, hope, and love.

May the God of hope fill you with all joy and peace as you trust in Him, so that you may overflow with hope by the power of the Holy Spirit.
- Romans 15:13

Chapter 1

Why This Book

Everything which lead up to the writing of this book originated with a question that I posed to myself and to God.

"Is pessimism a Biblical outlook?"

At first, this may seem like the last sort of question you would expect to ultimately culminate in a book focused on Biblical Hope. However, if I had been honest with myself at the time, or had a little more self-awareness, the actual question would have been "Isn't optimism the outlook a Christian should have?". The answer to both questions, surprisingly to me, was "No".

For many years I had been a self-described "hopeless optimist". The irony of that title is certainly not lost on me in hindsight. In all honesty, my original interest in beginning the study was to rebuke the pessimists in my life, and to provide them with the Biblical reasoning which proves why they should be more optimistic. Like me.

Having been raised to always prioritize the authority of Scripture, and to go to the Bible if I wanted to know the truth of how God would have me live and think, I turned to the Scriptures seeking validation for my worldview. Thankfully, the Word of God is always a reliable source of instruction, and the Holy Spirit is our faithful instructor.

"All Scripture is breathed out by God and profitable for teaching, for reproof, for correction, and for training in righteousness,"
2 Timothy 3:16 (ESV)

His power pierced my ego and His grace softened my heart. The process was not comfortable or quick, as it required constant submission to His authority and a willingness to keep nothing back as sacred.

If we want to be comfortable, we can never get too close to God. If we want to grow close to Him we have to be willing to be uncomfortable. We have to be willing to genuinely plead with the Spirit to search our hearts, *and* we must count nothing as so sacred that when He demands we turn it over to Him for destruction we withhold it. Because if there is any storied tradition or long-held belief that we are unwilling to submit to the testing of God, it is a obstacle; good for nothing other than to hinder our faith.

Sanctification can be a genuinely painful process, but if anything, no matter how precious, can be crushed under the weight of truth, then for our own good it must be.

What originated as a kind of thought experiment eventually morphed into an in-depth study of how we ought to approach the present circumstances and unknown future of our lives. Once it had become evident that God was not prescribing pessimism *or* optimism in the Scriptures, then that begged the question of "what *does* God command". There has to be a right way and a wrong way to frame our expectations in life. After all, there are express commands in the Bible of how *not* to think. Clearly the Word condemns a posture of anxiety and hopelessness. Whereas I supposed the righteous alternative to be optimism, which would validate my perceived godliness, what became equally and unavoidably clear is that optimism is in fact incompatible with a genuine and strong faith. So again I asked, this time without my own preconceived notions, what is the Christian perspective?

Hope.

Hope is greater than optimism, and is in fact what we are commanded to have throughout the Scriptures. It is the Biblical posture of our hearts and minds that we are to live in.

When this reality clicked for me and the truth of it began to work on my heart, I wanted to put it to the test. Because how often have we heard the con-men of the world and the church alike professing that they can give hope to the hopeless, only to be revealed as frauds because the hope that they offer is flimsy, circumstantial, and wholly insufficient? I do not want something that makes me feel good. I want something that puts the Rock of Ages beneath my feet; that though the storms and seas rail against me on all sides I will not be destroyed. Give me something real and powerful!

A hope worth having should be able to endure the most devastating events in our lives. It should be able to uplift and empower us to persevere to the very end. Too often the hope we are peddled is just optimism by a different name, or humanistic self-help which is little more than useless at best and grievously deceptive and harmful at its worst.

A hope like this is as necessary as it could ever be. When I began writing my first sermon notes in early 2019 I never would have imagined all that would transpire between then and now as I write this book. With each passing day, the message of Biblical Hope which I knew was needed then becomes more and more valuable.

We are in the throes of upheaval in the political, personal, and spiritual realms of our world at large. If we are to endure we will need hope of a mighty and eternal sort. Why should we settle for hope that lasts a moment, a few years, or even until we die? Would it not be better to have a hope of such eternal quality that it reaches even beyond the grave and into the life that is to come? Would you not rather have a hope that is beyond circumstance? One which is like the treasure Christ promised; which cannot be stolen, corrupted, or destroyed?[1] This is the hope that God has for us, and one that has unfortunately been missed by many Christians for many years. Now and always the need is great, and in God's goodness He

---

[1] Matthew 6:19-21

provides to meet the need.

It is by the Word of God that our Mighty Lord and Savior has revealed the truth of His nature to us. All of our troubles, fears, pains, and groanings can be brought to the Scriptures to find relief if we humble ourselves in submission to its ultimate authority over our lives. Likewise, all of our rejoicing, praises, and peace can find their origin, fashioning, and refinement within the pages of the Word of God. We can smell the breath of God in the pages of the Bible, and hear the rumblings of His voice.

God's hope cannot be overcome no matter our circumstances, backgrounds, or prospects. God's hope is not a carnal feeling of comfort or escape from our pain and darkness. The freedom He offers is not an escape at all; it is far greater. When we escape there is still a force that, if we were to fall into its clutches again, could enslave us once more. An escape is not victory over our enemy, only relief from their presence. Christ has secured victory for those who have called upon His name and received His grace and freedom.

Apart from God, we sink beneath the weight of our circumstances and drown in a perpetual current of despair. Many people, and even those who profess to have laid hold of the hope in Christ, adopt this model. They struggle all their days in an effort to keep themselves from drowning in the current as they are swept along to the Kingdom which awaits us at the end of it all.

We are equipped by our salvation to stand firm in the midst of the fiercest storms of woe which the world can offer. Because our feet are set firm on the unchanging nature of God, and His hand is against our back. Waves of misery may crash over us, but those who cling to the absolute character of God can remain steadfast against it all.

Bad news pours into our lives through every screen. Seemingly every conversation has some gravitational pull towards the bleak outlook which becomes more and more mainstream with each additional news story. We live in a time with unprecedented access to the miseries of the world. No longer are we permitted to concern ourselves with the burdens of our communities merely, but a responsibility is foisted on us to concern ourselves with every injustice, every monetary trouble, and every tribulation through an endless number of outlets. In a culture that has abandoned the pattern of interceding and laying pain and injustice at the feet of the Great Physician and Righteous Judge, we are left to shoulder the burdens of an entire world without a strategy for relief or renewal.

After a long day of gorging ourselves on information, we sleep fitfully and wake up to immediately flood our minds and hearts with more information and opinions than we could ever read, let alone process in any meaningful or fruitful way. This pattern continues, because it is what has been prescribed to us. You *must* have an opinion and a stance on *everything*. You *must* work as though you have been called to lead the masses which follow you on social media towards a brighter future. What arises is an error in our culture where we confuse *influence* with *anointing*, and this results in a great many people taking up a burden God never tasked them with or equipped them to carry.

This example is merely one of the myriad reasons why suicide and depression are so prevalent in our culture. In the wake of the 2020 Pandemic, depression in America climbed to affecting roughly 28% of Americans. Sadly, it has continued its climb, and some recent studies estimate that nearly 1 in 3 Americans now deal with depression[2]. 2019 had over 47,000 Americans end their lives with suicide[3]. Roughly 14 people out of every 100,000.

Some work to litigiously pick apart the "system" and rework it in such a way as to prevent the motivators for suicide. Others pursue spirituality and holistic living. Still others self-medicate as they work to soldier on with no prescription on how to actually be *free* of their burdens. Ultimately, everyone acknowledges that something is amiss, but they cannot agree on a way to repair it. However, there is revelation in Scripture which unveils

---

[2] Persistent Depressive Symptoms During Covid-19: A national, population-representative, longitudinal study of U.S. Adults - By: Catherine E. Ketman - Gregory H. Cohen - Salma M. Abdalla - Laura Sampson - Ludovic Trinquart - Brian C. Castrucci - et al. DOI: https://doi.org/10.1016/j.lana.2021.10091

[3] Ehlman DC, Yard E, Stone DM, Jones CM, Mack KA. Changes in Suicide Rates — United States, 2019 and 2020. MMWR Morb Mortal Wkly Rep 2022;71:306–312. DOI: http://dx.doi.org/10.15585/mmwr.mm7108a5external icon.

what we perceive in the flesh to be mere circumstance to actually be a consequence in the war against the powers of the present darkness of this age.

Our enemy is cunning and ruthless with a violent hatred for us. As such, he adjusts his strategies and tactics to suit the times we are in. 47,000 men, women, and children ended their lives in one country in one year! This is a loud cry from many that their hope has been lost. Men, women, and children who have surrendered themselves to the belief that if things change at all they will only become worse. They are snow-blind in the winter of their hearts and can no longer hope for spring to come.

The deep yearning in their soul has been dismissed by intellectuals and medicated by humanists. It has been pacified by watered down sermons, but it has not been satisfied.

We have a world filled with people who are born with a hunger for the divine and the eternal that will never be sated by _anything_ other than the divine and the eternal. In a world that has rejected God, we are left with entire nations of people who medicate and distract themselves from this yearning, and build fortresses for themselves on sinking sands so that if even the slightest gust comes against them they crumble.

How much more so will it fall under the duress of a global pandemic, civil unrest, or intense economic distress? When our walls are rattled so fiercely by the storms of life, as has been the case in recent years, even the Christian is tempted to fall into the trap of despair. We feel so completely overwhelmed that we throw up our hands in exasperation and cry, "Stop the world! I'm getting off.".

This is an unacceptable "solution". In such moments and dark days we must turn our eyes to Jesus as our Living Hope. We must lay hold of the Gospel, apply it to our lives, and watch as it transforms our reality. The true Word of God which upholds all of creation, and the blood of Christ which redeems all creation are more than capable of restoring hope to us, even in the midst of our most bitter trials.

In order to find this relief we have to be willing to step onto the battlefield and go to war with our enemy. We cannot expect to be permitted to rest in cozy bunkers built with the theological revelations of the fathers and mothers of our faith. They are still just as true today as they were then, and just as useful for our sanctification and preservation as they were when the Holy Spirit first revealed them. God has not changed, and His truth is still as powerful, relevant, and effective for ministering to the despairing believer and unbeliever alike.

You may ask, "Why then do we need to continue pursuing revelation and step out from the comfort of these traditions, if they are still so potent?". My answer to this question comes in two parts. One focusing centrally on our enemy, and the other focusing on the Church itself.

Firstly, we must remember that Satan is not God. He is not all-knowing or all-powerful and as such his strategies of attack change throughout the ages as he works to destroy God's people. There are seasons where it may seem that the enemy has outpaced our defenses with his attacks and that the Church itself is at the cusp of being entirely destroyed, but God can never be outwitted or outmaneuvered. His design from the beginning is to use the overwhelming attacks of Satan and the subsequent pain to lead His people into greater spiritual maturity and strength.

We must also remember that the Church itself is built upon two thousand years of continuous revelation. God has given us everything we need in His Living Word. It is eternally infallible and unchanging. There is no cultural context which can render any part of its truth irrelevant. Yet we are being "made ready" by His Holy Spirit who was sent as our great helper in these last days[4]. Christ's Church was not established by the Spirit as a completed project. In much the same way that a parent is not given a complete and perfect human in their newborn baby, who they are merely tasked with screwing up as little as possible until they are an adult and set off on their own. Parents are given a child who they must work hard to love and guide towards maturity. They are given raw un-tailored life which must then be shaped into a kind and good person.

---

[4] Revelation 19: 7-10

At Pentecost, the Holy Spirit gave the world a Church in its infancy. Now, by His faithful hand the Church is two thousand years old. Scripture says that He is preparing the bride and making her perfect for the day Christ returns for His people so that she might be presented holy and blameless before Him. Now, I do not see God as someone who cares much for looking busy. He certainly wouldn't send His Spirit to work on making perfect something that was already perfect.

I am *not* saying that we currently have influences equal to that of the Holy Spirit divinely inspiring the writing of Scripture. I *am* saying that two millennia of the Holy Spirit revealing the hidden truths He concealed within His Word until the body would reach a time of maturity to receive them is an awfully long time. Just think of how much a person changes in the time between their first and twentieth birthdays. The Lord is not limited by the constraints of time and understanding, but we are. He has patiently taught what Christians have needed centuries to grasp.

I would submit to you that the modern Church more closely resembles the fullness of God's vision for His Kingdom than the first century Church. Peoples of every tribe, every tongue, and every nation cry out that Jesus is Lord! Individuals gather in stadiums and in homes to be found in every corner of the Earth to worship Him. The Holy Spirit has lovingly fostered the Church and grown her in righteousness unto where the Christian

Church has been instrumental in the continued dignifying of every human and the cultural value placed on human life.

Rejoice then that God is perfecting the bride!

All of this serves as the foundation to answer the question, "Why am I writing this book?". Ultimately, the answer is so that people who read it may better know God. Not just that they would know *about* Him, but that they would know Him in the intimate manner that He desires to be known by us. To know Him as the loving Heavenly Father who we can come to with all our needs. To know Him as the waiting Bridegroom who patiently pursues His wayward bride. To know Him as the Great Helper who works within us to bring about His eternal kingdom and to pull back the scales from our eyes so that we may fully behold His glory and the wonder of His ways.

When we truly know God, not as we want Him to be, but as He has revealed Himself to be, we cannot help but to have hope. What other response could possibly be suitable in light of such a mighty, good, and loving God?

Still, hope and peace both seem to be such slippery prospects in our modern lives. The sobering reality of this world is that as long as the current world order persists, that is until Christ returns and fully manifests His Kingdom here on Earth, there will be anger, wrath, violence, injustice, pain, and terrifying darkness. We who have been redeemed by Christ live as aliens in a kingdom of evil. It should never be expected that a life lived with and for Christ will be free from trials or tribulations. Christ actually *promises* that we will be hated and rejected and even killed for His namesake. [5] The eternal kingdom and peace forevermore are promised only on the other side of the valley of death. One might wonder, why does Christ not immediately call His beloved children into His arms at their conversion? Why does He will that they should have to suffer and endure in a broken world?

Because we cannot shine a light into darkness we are not walking through. What good is a lantern under a bushel when there are those yet wandering and lost in the darkness?[6] How would the Samaritan have found the man beaten and bloodied on the side of the road, mere inches from death, if he himself had not been walking the treacherous path?[7]

So, this book is not a topical balm to ease your worry and reassure you that if you follow a magical formula and memorize a few key verses the troubles that surround you will be turned away. It is certainly not a promise that you will no longer need to defend your hope or your peace from the enemy. It is my prayer that this book will be a helpful reinforcement to you as you tarry on in this present darkness.[8] That as we explore God's Word, and the

---

[5] Matthew 5:44

[6] Matthew 5:15

[7] Luke 10:25-37

[8] Ephesians 6:12

mighty truths that reside therein, we will be emboldened in our mission by a flow of Heavenly Hope! That it will burn brightly inside of us and bring us peace that surpasses all understanding.

Perhaps you have walked with the Lord for many years, and still wonder where your hope is. Maybe the world has trodden you under its heel and you are torn as to whether or not God's love does actually give us lasting reason for hope. You may be a young believer, newborn in the faith, and you are wondering where this living hope you were promised can be found. Wherever you turn your eyes in your daily life you feel a cold knot of despair in your stomach that has replaced the fire you felt at your conversion. Your mind may feel drawn to doubts, and a fear of unbelief has crept into your heart. Or you may be a believer in any walk of life, and you *know* there is hope to be found in Christ, if only you knew where to look. You have listened to sermon after sermon, read all the material you can lay your hands on, but the answers you uncover seem ill-suited for the worry in your life. Some may be long-time friends of the Lord and are searching for a loving reminder of His Hope to fill their sails.

In this book, I want to address the hard and frightening questions we must face when dealing with the subject of eternal hope. Rather than shying away, we *must* shine the light of Scripture on them. In so doing, I believe that this book will be of use to anyone who desires hope; regardless of the state of their walk with God. I believe that the Holy Spirit greatly desires to rekindle the hope of His people, so that we can shine a light in a darkened world. One which cannot be concealed or snuffed out by suffering. Christ has sent us into the world, and the Holy Spirit equips us to go. Right now the world we are sent to is in desperate need of hope, and we are the ones tasked with delivering it. Blessed are the feet of those who bring the good news![9]

The Hope God offers is transformative. Not just for us, but for our culture as well. It radically changes the way things work because it is a system and pattern of the Kingdom of Heaven. It is a taste of the fast-approaching restoration of God's perfect created order.[10] That we may find ourselves at any moment and in any circumstance rooted in hope and peace that confounds understanding.[11] Everyone of us is in need of something or someone that we can rely on no matter what. We can seek our security in material things, relationships, or self-reliance, but everything on this Earth will ultimately fall short and fail us.

God has provided us with a hope that is without failure or blemish. There is a foundation available for our hope that can and will bear up under the most intense scrutiny or the weightiest opposition. There will never be a moment where we cannot cast the full weight of our pain and despair on the Rock of Ages and find that He is not up to the task. As we will see.

---

[9] Romans 10:14-15
[10] Matthew 17:11

[11] Philippians 4:6

Chapter 2

Defining Terms

Words are incredibly important. Growing up, my parents hammered home for me that it is never all about what we say, but *exactly* what we say. Modern American culture is a prime example of why taking time to define and outline the terms you plan to use is incredibly important. Not only have recent years involved the mixing, matching, and fashioning of words, as well as the redefinition of long agreed upon terms in order to suit politically acceptable messaging, but even words such as justice, reconciliation, and accountability (words often defined by and directly associated with the Church) have been expanded and repurposed to mean innumerable things. While it may be impossible to all be on the same page in society at large, we can at least do so for the purposes of this book.

For the purposes of this book, the primary terms I want to take the time to define are Secular Realism, Sacred Realism, Optimism, Pessimism, and Hope. Notice that I have uniquely divided Realism into Secular and Sacred (Christian) categories. While considering the topics covered in this book I found myself more and more convinced that Realism is segmented into these two opposing schools of thought, hinging upon the simple question of what one believes about God. The differences that arise are not subtle in either the theoretical or practical senses, and we would benefit from looking at both individually rather than as a whole.

Secular Realism

Humans are by our very nature subjective in everything that we do. There is an ever-present influence which impacts our decision-making in any given scenario. Even a desire to be objective will ultimately subjectify our decision making because that desire must be coupled with our understanding in order for us to choose what we *believe to be* objective.

As an example, if you have a friend coming into town and they are interested in trying the local fare, you may be tempted to take them to your favorite restaurant. However, if you are trying to be objective about the quality, you may know that your favorite restaurant is not necessarily the best one around. So instead you try to be objective and think of which dining experience trumps the others. Flavor, service, quality of ingredients, and menu complexity may all be factors to consider. At the end of the day though these objective standards will have to be interpreted through your own subjective tastes. For this reason, I would argue again that any person who has feelings, whose emotions can be influenced for or against any object or subject at all, and who is honest with themselves will find that they are incapable of being a *pure* realist.

How then do we go about addressing realism? Is it dissolved by the existence of a subjective leaning present in every person's heart and mind? Not necessarily. In fact there are innumerable factors which weigh in on our perceptions and decision-making in any given moment! However, there is one such factor which is so fundamentally influential, so transformative, that it gives us our plumb line by which we can take billions of individual worldviews and generalize them into two major categories.

What do you believe about God?

Not, "Do you believe *in* God?", but "What do you believe *about* Him?". More specifically, do you believe that He is living, good, present, and active? Or do you believe in whole or in part that He is cruel, dead, small, or gone/entirely removed? This dividing line affects even the realist, perhaps more than they may ever realize or admit. Because, when you factor into consideration every bit of relevant information concerning a circumstance, and selectively omit the Father you are far more likely to despair than you are to rejoice. What reason do you have to be hopeful or positive when presented with the smallness of your might, the horror of your opposition, and the absence of an Almighty God?

Even our most staunchly atheist intellectuals will readily admit that the world is a mess. Those who possess even a passing shadow of understanding will not be able to escape this truth, especially if they intend to look at things as they are and not allow themselves to fall into denial. Entire systems of government are built upon the exploitation and oppression of the people under their care. Starvation, poverty, and slavery persist in even some of the most developed nations. While some of the ugliness in our world remains in the shadows, in our information age much of it is on display for all to see.

A curse accompanies natural knowledge without faith. In much the same way that Adam and Eve ate the forbidden fruit of the tree of the knowledge of good and evil and were cursed with what they sought. Their sinful rejection of God's authority and divine knowledge left them outside of the grace of His garden where they once had everything they would ever need. They obstinately landed themselves in an inhospitable land. Where once dominion was a mantle laid on their shoulders by the Creator, now they would have to labor by the sweat of their brow to "subdue" an Earth which would fight against them until the curse is at last removed[12].

This horrible state of affairs is the same one that a secular realist who forsakes the truth of God's divine authority and nature finds themselves married to. Because the curse of a broken and fallen world has not been removed, we are still fragile creatures who are burdened with the ability to discern what great forces oppose us, and lack the power to claim victory over them.

Most, if not all, people will feel the incredible weight of the current world order pressed against us and we are made keenly aware of our helplessness in the face of its might. We are incapable of dictating even the smallest

---

[12] Genesis 3

details of our lives against forces such as governments, natural disasters, culture, or time itself. Anyone who strives to be a realist under such weight will inevitably find that despair and negativity begin to have a nearly irresistible draw.

This is where the line between Secular Realism and Pessimism eventually begins to blur, to a point where they are essentially indistinguishable from one another, in practice. For example, how many times have you heard someone in your life being pessimistic and throwing out the old canned response, "Listen, I'm just trying to be a realist here."? I would argue that a realist is just a pessimist who is optimistic that they are *not* a pessimist.

Unfortunately this mindset of denying or excluding God's revealed nature can be found in the hearts and minds of many professing Christians as well. This is why the question at the beginning of this chapter goes beyond simply, "Do you believe in God?" and hinges instead on what you believe *about* God. There are those who claim salvation in Christ who otherwise put little stock in who God has said He is. In the broader public arena, there are influential speakers who claim that the express commands of Scripture are largely open for reinterpretation within the popular deconstructionist movement. This is the current wave of conflicted professing Christians who rethink their faith and either remove core elements which they no longer approve of and rework the revealed truths of God found in Scripture to suit their sensibilities or dispose of their faith altogether.

At times they go so far as to claim as truth, theories about God's character which are in direct opposition to what He has revealed of Himself in no uncertain terms.

The plain speech of Scripture to such people is little more than a bargain bin of feel-good messages that they can sift through and accessorize with when they see fit. Anything that does not fall in line with their own understanding is tossed aside.

This skewed view of the God of Scriptures, if they believe in the God of the Bible in the first place, is a crippling wound to the faith and hope of a professing Christian. It hamstrings the runner and hinders them from running the race well. They throttle their own faith, and are quick to error when they substitute out God as He has revealed Himself for God as they suppose Him to be. When we allow ourselves to believe in a small, distant, or otherwise uninvolved God, our faith can very easily become polluted by a "Christianized" version of Secular Realism. Because a God who is not the God of Scripture is no better, in many respects, than no God at all.

Sacred Realism

Whereas the Secular Realist inevitably finds themselves drawn towards pessimism, the Realist who places their faith in the God of the Bible as the defining element of their worldview will find themselves pressed beyond simple optimism and into extravagant hope. God gives birth to hope in our hearts and minds because of who He is and how He is at work in our lives.

Whereas a life in a Godless universe is devoid of any genuine or lasting reason for hope, there is no valid response other than hope when the truth of God's nature invades and shapes your reality.

Secular Realism is in many ways synonymous or at least indistinguishable from pessimism, and so too is Sacred Realism synonymous with Hope. This mentality and worldview is potent and capable of establishing a "positive outlook" that will endure hardships far longer than anything Optimism might provide. Hope is only as strong as whatever it is built upon. So the desire of the realist, to be objective and forsake the ignorance that many use to shield and preserve fragile happiness, can be satisfied in Biblical Hope. Additionally, our natural yearning and supernatural groanings for hope and for joy which cause our very souls to ache can be satisfied. The appetite of our souls finds its contentment in the Bread of Life, of which we eat and never hunger again[13].

Sacred Realism does require much from our faith if it is to be of any benefit to ourselves or to others. This is not an indictment on the idea, nor is it proof that it does not qualify as Realism. First, it requires that we genuinely look at our lives with all the warts and trials. Do not ever turn your eyes away from the ugliness of your life in fear that God is not good enough to deliver you from it! Second, we must search out the nature of God in the pages of His Holy Scriptures, and then we *must take Him at His Word.*

---

[13] John 6:35

God's Word is either entirely true or it is entirely discredited. So we must be willing to apply the truth of God's righteous character to even the most desperate of circumstances, and walk with faith if we want to see the consequences of His nature at work in our lives.

Anything short of complete honesty with our circumstances, and complete belief in the God of the Bible will leave us with a half-measure of peace and a flimsy optimism dressed up as hope. This was the head space I found *myself* in once I turned to Scripture for support of optimism and the condemnation of pessimism.

As I progressed in adulthood and was faced with real world opposition, I became increasingly dissatisfied with the "peace" provided by simply ignoring what was wrong in my world because being ignorant and happy was better than being informed and depressed. The natural question which followed, and which I now pose to the reader if you find yourself in a similar situation is, "What small version of God do I believe in, that His goodness must be shielded from my hardships in order to preserve the peace and joy He promises?" Do you quarantine the character of God from your trials in life as though He is capable of being soiled by them?

The God of Scripture is one who promises persecution and *in the same breath* tells His disciples, "Do not worry about anything[14]". If you take the

---

[14] Matthew 5:43-48 and Matthew 6:25-34

Bible at its word you are given a picture of a God whose goodness, peace, joy, and hope are actually impervious enough to weather any tragedy, complex enough to benefit even the most uniquely tried believer, and powerful enough to not only be present in but even to be sovereignly worked out *through* our suffering.

Once faith allows us to lay hold of this divine knowledge, our grasp of reality now made full, we cannot help but find ourselves filled with the Hope of Christ!

Pessimism and Optimism

While Pessimism and Optimism have already been alluded to briefly in the previous sections, I think it is still worth fleshing out the definitions a bit more, albeit briefly as we will look at both in depth later in the book. The core of both belief systems can be boiled down once again to the fateful question, "What do you believe about God?". There are seldom extravagant differences between a professing believer or a staunch atheist who fall into either worldview, as both parties arrive at the same school of thought, be it optimism or pessimism, just by different roads.

Pessimism in this book will be referring to an outlook on life in its past, present, and future state which is predominantly negative. This is modeled by the "3 P's of Pessimism". These are Personalization, Pervasiveness, and Permanence. A pessimist believes that negative circumstances in their life have been done to them personally, that these things spill over from one area of their life and cause all other parts of their life to be negatively impacted, and that this will continue on with no end in sight.

Oftentimes a pessimist will use negative situations in their lives and levy them as evidence against the character of God. If they are so far removed from their naturally occurring wisdom so as to deny God entirely, they will phrase it as it just being the way life is. Unfortunately, pessimists rarely find themselves at a loss for circumstantial evidence to support their claim, and will further entrench themselves in the belief.

A pessimist believes that they have managed to see a situation for what it truly is, and that they simply refuse to buy into a willful ignorance in order to preserve the illusion of positivity. The truth of the matter is that they are actually half right! Happiness or positivity that cannot hold up under the weight of truth is weak and worse than useless. Anything that we believe in which requires ignorance is not going to be worth believing in at all. If it can be destroyed under the weight of truth, then it deserves to be. Where pessimism falls woefully short is that it trades an ignorance built to avoid reality for an ignorance built to cope with reality. The pessimist elevates their tribulations to equal footing with the promises of Scripture and in so doing they rob themselves of the riches of faith.

Optimism, conversely, is an outlook on life in its past, present, and future state which is predominantly positive. For most people, especially in relatively wealthy and developed countries, optimism will be sufficient throughout much of their lives. This is coming from a former relatively comfortable optimist. Problems arise when blind positivity is genuinely challenged by real life circumstances which cannot be covered, ignored, or bypassed. General cheerfulness and the stubborn belief that everything will work out alright, or that it's never as bad as it seems, does little in the face of actual suffering. When the optimist is met by these challenges they will find themselves pressed to an ultimatum. Either they succumb to despair, or they choose to be willfully ignorant of the severity of the difficulty. The latter is attractive because if being sorrowful or happy will not affect the outcome either way, we would rather be happy.

If Realism is the cousin of Pessimism, then Optimism is the counterfeit of Hope. Very rarely will we find Optimism to be a satisfactory solution to the deeper agonies of life. It amateurishly mimics the effects of Hope while lacking any of the substance or vitality. In seasons of deep trouble we are made painfully aware of how flimsy a shield Optimism becomes when you are tasked with actually *solving* problems and not just *surviving* them.

A fitting illustration of this difference would be to imagine the windshield in your car. You can see all of your surroundings through it, and it protects you from many typical hazards. Yet there is no substitute for a seat-belt if you are in a car crash. A bad enough collision will throw you from your car, straight through your windshield which previously offered such satisfactory defense. That which you trusted to protect you is wholly inadequate to the task and is of no help to you in your time of need.

We do not need an outlook that shields us from discomfort. We need a hope that will save us from destruction.

Hope

Biblical Hope and its application is the core theme and end goal of this book. Whenever I refer to Hope it is in the context of what can be found and confirmed in Scripture. It is not a fuzzy warm feeling, nor a hope that is built on circumstances, people, or resources. The Hope I am referring to is not natural or earthly, but supernatural and holy.

Our natural definition of hope is, "A desire with expectation of obtainment or fulfillment".[15] However, this makes no mention of the source of hope. What is it that gives validity to this feeling of expectation?

Our greater Hope in Christ springs from an assurance of the nature of a Holy God which impacts our reality and informs our expectations. We are able to place our hope not just in an expected outcome, but in an outcome that has been guaranteed by the blood purchase of Jesus Christ. We have expectations because the ever faithful and unchanging God of the Universe has made promises which in Christ are all yes and amen. Again I remind us

---

[15] Merriam-Webster Dictionary

that our hope is only ever as strong as whatever it is built upon.

As cultural norms have integrated themselves into the Church at large. As fierce and convicted preaching on the absolute authority and inerrancy of Scripture has waned. We have seen such Hope fade in the life of the average believer. I believe that such robust and unshakable Hope is one of the prizes that Christ bought for us at the cross, and eternally secured at His resurrection. It ought to dramatically impact our lives, our faith, our churches, and the culture itself. It is a facet of the culture found in the Kingdom of Heaven, the same Kingdom which we are tasked with bringing to Earth in our time here.

By God's grace we will explore how this Hope is unique and effective in application. So that we may walk in the riches of His grace as co-heirs with Christ.

Chapter 3

My God is He: Pessimism

Can a Christian who obeys the Word of God find approval in its pages to be a pessimist? As you may have guessed from the title of the book and from reading so far, I have not found a Biblical foundation for pessimism in Scripture.

The unfortunate and deceptive nature of pessimism is such that it keeps us near-sighted, and closed-minded to the authority of Scripture. Pessimists are convinced that they are merely being realistic about not only their circumstances, but the nature of life itself. This is only made all the worse when well-meaning people attempt to downplay the severity of their situation. Empty assurances are given that it surely cannot ever be as bad as it seems, and that everything must work out in the end. Arguments that things are not as bad as they seem and will eventually get better are flimsy, often untrue, and seldom Biblical. They are weak substitutes for hope, intended to cushion and shield us from the discomfort of facing our issues directly and faithfully, and most often they fall short in changing a despairing pessimist's mind. Pessimists despair because they feel it is *warranted* by their circumstances and experiences.

What we must be careful of when trying to lift our brother out of despair, or shake the chains of pessimism off our own hearts, is that we do not trivialize the pain in an attempt to magnify God. In doing so you will not have glorified the King of Heaven and Earth, but will instead have worked to defend a god of your own design from that which threatens to dismantle him.

When we turn to Scripture we are met with story after story of Biblical characters afflicted with all manners of suffering and how they respond to God in the midst of it. Searching these stories, what we will not find is God condoning His people to remain in despair. One of the most famous examples, and the primary focus of this chapter, is the life of Job.

Job was a righteous man blessed with wealth and status, and in the span of a single day it was all ripped away from him. If anyone ever had just cause to remain forever in despair, it would be Job. Instead, we find that Job managed to stave off his negativity for a season. Though he did grieve and mourn as was fitting for his state of affairs, he provides a stark contrast to the reader in parallel to his wife who immediately yielded to her pain and circumstances. He resisted the draw of despair even when she told him to curse God and die.

It is exceedingly easy when we look and see trouble on all sides to feel crushed by the weight of our pain. The demons in our life howl and crowd our vision, piling fact upon fact in front of us until we cannot help but feel the need to hold them in the same regard as the truth of Scripture. When our family is torn apart by divorce. When a job is suddenly lost and our sense of financial security evaporates. When loved ones are subjected to terrible violence. In these moments for the believer who does not wish to let go of God, we may instead decide that He must be less loving, less involved, less good, less righteous, less powerful, less Godly than He has claimed to be.

This was the view of Job's wife, and eventually Job himself. Such is the manner of the pessimist.

In Chapters 29 and 30 of the book of Job, the titular character recounts the beautiful life he once led. He did not minimize or romanticize the life he treasured before. These were the facts of the life that he had lost so violently. Once he was a man of high honor, who counseled rulers and young men alike. His wealth was extravagant and was matched by his generosity. Before God he was blameless; an upright and righteous man who kept His Lord's commands. The contrast we find in these chapters is stark. Job's name, in his lowly state, had become a slur and a curse. He was utterly rejected by even his closest friends and kin, as they hurled accusation after accusation upon him without evidence other than his already pitiful state.

Rarely will you find anyone who has suffered as deeply as Job does in his story. Wonderfully, the pressing of Job is not solely to convict the complainer, although is certainly one aspect of it, but also so that each of us who has felt similar pain may read and see how God deals with His servant who is pushed to the utmost. No one is spared from seasons of trouble, or winters of the heart that browbeat us and tempt us to despair. Many have experienced going from living their life with vigor and joy, to being struck down and trampled underfoot. When once still waters now seem to flow against you with all their might and steal everything away in their rolling waves. In those moments we are deeply tempted to despair! Our flesh demands that we curse God and die. Yet it is even here, before we reach the culmination of Job's story, while he is still in the depths of his suffering that we find a clear opposition to pessimism in the form of Job's rebuke to his wife.

Whereas his wife bade him to lash out in fury against his God and in defiance give up his hold on life itself, Job instead fell onto his knees in the midst of his grief and *worshiped* God.

His wife's reply to this outpouring of praise to the Father is one that is not uncommon to find when people are the victims of hardship. "Why worship God if this is where it gets you?" How many times have these words, this lie, been believed? The lie that we can somehow put God on trial against standards we have set for Him and deem Him unworthy of our worship if our life doesn't match what we expected. What *is* uncommon is the response Job offers in return. He called this disbelief exactly what it is.

Foolishness.

A willingness only to accept what is *pleasant* from God, and then to withhold our praise from Him in the midst of hardship throws light on idols hiding in the shadows of our hearts. It betrays a twisted view of God, in which we have delicately pieced together the deity we are willing to serve and revere.

Because when we reject God in our discomfort and in our suffering, it is revealed that we have made a god of our comfort. Once that comfort disappears, so too does our worship and our confidence.

By worshiping in the midst of his heart-rending grief Job refused to relegate the God of the Universe to a means to his own ends. This does not mean that Job's suffering was not genuine, excruciating, or tragic. He had lost everything, save his life. We do not need to minimize our suffering in order to reconcile it to God's nature. If the God you believe in cannot survive the dire circumstances of your life, then you do not believe in the God of Scripture the way that you ought to. Those who succumb to despair and attempt to call God to account rather than seek shelter in His arms have fallen victim to their own perverted notions of His character. They know that God has said He is good, He is love, and that He is faithful; however, their understanding of what that *means in practice* is twisted by their natural knowledge.

Natural or carnal knowledge tells us that good *feels* good, and God's goodness must follow suit. Again, through our fleshly and natural understanding, love is gentle and comfortable when it is proper. Faithfulness in leadership means that the leader offers transparency and that their methods are understandable and beneficial. It interprets the promises of God through "want", and therefore makes our temperament the authority on God's provision. In turn we fashion a small version of God in our hearts and minds whose integrity is tied to our own understanding. We begin to look at God's nature through the lens of our circumstances rather than interpreting our circumstances through the lens of God's truth.

Ultimately this leads, as we see with even Job towards the end of the story, to bitterness towards God. Even the most upright and righteous man of his time will find it hard to withstand the constant diminishing that suffering brings. Especially when little by little his gaze turns inward, his vision becomes cluttered by his trials, and he begins to lean on his own understanding.

Have you ever found yourself in a similar situation? Where you once began your testing season strong and full of faith, but over time finding that your faith has worn thin. Where the waves of life have buffeted you, and it feels like every time you get a breath and think you see land on the horizon another swell crashes overhead and threatens to drown you. Every time a gut punch takes the wind out of you, you find it harder to gasp your praises to God, and those praises become questions, and those questions become accusations. Know that you are not alone.

It is not difficult for suffering to blossom into doubting. Like Job, we are prone to feeling slighted by God. Because our limited understanding, warped by our pain, cannot seem to reconcile God to our suffering. We find ourselves bitterly complaining, "God may be good, but He hasn't been good to *me*.". We become blinded by our circumstances and we cry foul against the God of the Universe for abandoning us to our troubles.

Growing up, I had a bewildering natural talent for standing in the exact right location and in the exact right position to deftly block my parent's view of the television. They wanted to watch the game winning touchdown? Too bad, I watched it instead! They wanted to watch the epic final battle, where evil falls and good triumphs? Well I did too, so that's just too bad. In these instances, I received a sarcastic compliment without fail.

"Son, you make a better door than a window."

They were, of course, entirely correct. I was much better at blocking a view than I was at providing one. In the same way, we can search this portion of Job's lament and get some clue into why he was overcome by despair. Pulling on this thread reveals a telling truth as to how the enemy can confound us and shackle us with negativity.

Our pain makes a better door than a window.

Do not be confused when your brother or sister is not uplifted when you try to point to what God is doing in the midst of their circumstances. Often you would be better off asking a blindfolded person to simply open their eyes and see the rays of sunlight chasing away the night. There are times when looking at our circumstances, we can see the hand of God and our spirits will be lifted. Other times the scorching heat of our pain is blinding and fills our vision to where it is impossible to make out the shape of anything other than the source of our suffering. In those moments our hurt is so deep that we are at a loss to be able to believe that there is anything other than the pain. We peer with feeble eyes and wrestle with the infinite will of God with our finite understanding. There will be many times in our lives where the evidence of God's work and presence in the midst of our trials is beyond our perception or comprehension.

"When His lamp shone upon my head, and by His light I walked through darkness, as I was in my prime, when the friendship of God was upon my tent, when the Almighty was yet within. When my children were all around me."
Job 29:3-5 (ESV)

Job became convinced that the Lord had departed from him. He looked around at the ruins of his life, and determined that he was lost in the darkness; that the light of the Lord no longer dwelled with him. Job tasted the bitterness of illness and felt the sting of loss, and he supposed that Jehovah had forsaken his friendship and turned him over to his anguish. I would hazard a guess that almost anyone motivated to pick up this book at all will have felt this way at some point in their lives. In the midst of such intense pain our grief may overwhelm us until the embers of faith are all but extinguished.

"By His light I walked through darkness"

God's Word is the light which shines at our feet[16], illuminating each step so that we do not stumble in the darkness. By His grace we navigate the snares and pitfalls which would cast us headlong on our path. Yet how often will the grumbler fail to see any light in its pages? It is natural for the mind, mired in troubles, to assume that the oil has run out of this holy lantern. Or worse still, they may find themselves believing that it has been covered, and the Holy Spirit has left them to stumble in darkness. One could suppose that God has left them to grope in the darkness until at last they see the light of His golden shores and find relief.

Make no mistake, we do walk in an age of darkness; in a broken and fallen world which opposes the Father of Lights[17]. So now, as we are sojourners

---

[16] Psalm 119:105
[17] James 1:17

here for a season, God has given us His Word as a beacon of the divine light. Whenever we open its pages, the light of God spills forth because His very nature is documented there in ink and paper. In the Holy Writ the unsearchable God has made Himself known. If there is a present darkness, and there is *also* an uncompromising light, then those who find themselves unable to perceive the blinding radiance of the Lord of lords can likely attribute it to one of a few possible reasons.

1. The darkness has overcome the light.
2. They have not yet accessed the source of the light.
3. Something is preventing them from seeing the light.

The light of the Word cannot be overcome. As John 1 teaches us, the Word (Jesus) is the light which shines in the darkness and is not overcome[18]. Even in our most dire straits we cannot suppose that the light of the world has been overcome. His victory has been sure since before the foundations of the Earth[19], and is the outpouring of a power like no other.

While the second option is certainly a possibility, especially in the life of an unbeliever who has perhaps never gone to God's Word for their hope, it is not the situation that we see exemplified for us in the story of Job. A non-Christian may very well find that turning to God and His Word will

---

[18] John 1:5
[19] Revelation 13:8

immediately shine light in their life that they never thought possible. Even a backslidden Christian who professes belief in Christ, but who has not submitted themselves to the teachings and authority given by God for our good, will often find themselves blinded by the brilliant light once the dust is brushed off and the pages are opened.

However, what we see in the case of Job is often the case for the downtrodden believer. He bemoans how the lamp of the Lord no longer shines on him. Job knows where to turn for his comfort, and yet he finds none. When he turns to the Word of the Lord he finds his darkness unchanged and receives no light by which he can choose his next steps. This leads me to believe that he has fallen prey to the third and final option; that something has managed to prevent him from seeing the light. We find our evidence of this in the telling end of the passage we listed.

"When my children were all around me."

While this is but a small snippet of the passage seemingly tacked onto the very end, it actually brings clarity to the claims which led up to it. A righteous and lawful man such as Job would know that the lamp of the Lord cannot be veiled or extinguished. He ought to also know that God does not merely abandon His friends to their demise and cut them off from Himself without warning or cause. Even the foulest and most wretched sinners, who defame and blaspheme the Lord, are given multiple opportunities to humble themselves and repent. This should be telling for us when we find a seasoned brother or sister in Christ, whose knowledge of the Word we have admired and whose life is in keeping with truth, and they falter in their hope. They may even make accusations against the nature of God when we know with certainty that the quality of their faith would normally not permit them to believe such lies. Because once we look at this last portion we see that Job is actually looking at the nature of God through his suffering rather than the other way around.

Job's children *were* taken from him suddenly and violently. This is a fact. Yet facts are not truth. Even the oldest and most universally recognized facts to be found in creation have their beginning point. For instance, the earth was once shapeless and void, and then it wasn't. That would be considered the genesis of the *fact* that the Earth is formed and full of life. All of creation was once perfect, and in perfect communion with its creator God, and now it is at odds with Him. However, there is a day where that fact too will reach its end because Christ's sacrifice and God's redeeming work are eternal *truth*, are without beginning or end, and will ultimately reform the facts of all creation. Facts all have a beginning and will ultimately either change or come to an end. Facts are the handles by which we try to grip the truth and are only as useful as our understanding permits them to be.

Truth is formative while facts are informative.

Where the pessimist and/or the despairing believer errs is in turning this order around. They elevate the facts, as they understand them, above the truth of God. In so doing their eyes are blinded by what they have decided to focus on, and they are unable to see the light available to them. This conflict is a hinge-point moment for many people. Some relieve the tension between their beliefs and their circumstances by turning to a more palatable God. One who is either too small or too distant to affect their circumstances, thus making His existence easier to reconcile with their pain. Others find the taste of God's nature and sovereignty to be too bitter, and like a child who gags on the wine of the covenant they spit Him out of their lives altogether.

In our generally comfortable and relatively affluent culture we have little issue believing in a God who is all powerful, but at a comfortable distance. The world is filled with powers-that-be which are far beyond us and they often remain impersonal. I know that there are elected and appointed officials who run my country and who wield incredible power. I know *of them* but I do not know them on any personal level. Why would I balk at the idea of an omnipotent God so much greater than I am, and far from my reach? Likewise, it is almost no trouble at all to believe in a God who is loving and friendly towards us. One who is genuinely good and desires our good. There is more than enough beauty and happiness in this world to display the tender hand of a loving creator.

The tension of God is held in that He is all powerful *and* all good. Not merely in spite of suffering and trials, but through them as well. We cannot make the one true God smaller than He is, because a god who *cannot* help me beyond what I am able to do for myself is not worthy of my worship. Why should we entrust our lives to a god who cannot defend or rescue us? Neither can we make God distant in our minds. A god who has withdrawn from us into the furthest reaches of the heavens, and is neither loving nor tender towards us, who is cold and far from influencing anything in our lives with personal intention is as good as no god at all.

By making God smaller He becomes a "little g" god. A deaf, mute, blind, and impotent idol. By making God distant we become godless, because why would we expect the fulfillment of promises made of provision and salvation by a God who does not care for us?

While the pessimist can be blinded by their circumstances in the negative sense, as illustrated, they can also be blinded in the positive sense. In the negative, they suppose that we are without God and He has abandoned us. In the positive, they suppose that we deserve and have merited His action on our behalf. Turning again to Job, we can see an example of this kind of thinking in his outcry against the Lord in Job 29:18.

"Then I thought, "I shall die in my nest, and I shall multiply my days as the sand.""

I shall.

Because of righteous deeds, because I'm a good person, because I have done so much for God and His people "I shall" receive the promised rewards of God. I have *earned* a long and happy life! This man's complaint to God serves to condemn his own belief system. How often do we find ourselves in a similar situation? Where our anger towards God finds its foundation in a belief that we can somehow earn from Him. Or that we can somehow indebt Him to us.

Pessimists place God on trial for how *they* expected Him to fulfill *His* promises. Be careful not to assume that this mentality does not apply to your own dealings with God. It is not relegated to the self-righteous alone. Whether we believe in our own worthiness or our own worthlessness, this is a deadly poison to our faith. Because, when things do not go how we expect them to, the former takes it as evidence that God's true nature is that of a cheat towards His obedient children, and the latter takes it as the cold chastisement of a God whom they can never hope to please. Once we adopt this outlook, it is nefariously self-perpetuating. This is one of the great dangers of pessimism.

Pessimism feeds on misfortune and disappointment. It is never short on what it needs to constantly confirm itself. Solidifying itself as an unassailable fact of life, in the pessimist's mind.

Pessimism tempts its target with promises of clarity and enlightenment. Many who despair believe that rather than being blinded by their pain and circumstances their reality has actually been illuminated by them. Pessimism does not provide enlightenment, rather it makes us near-sighted and reactionary. To the pessimist, the Biblical reply is given by Job earlier in the book. "You speak as one of those without understanding."

In all of our agony and suffering it is foolishness to not place our hope in the Lord. You may ask, "How do I acknowledge the reality of my pain and not succumb to the grumbling of pessimism?". We must shipwreck our pessimism against the nature of God. Your suffering is valid, and God was good long before you were ever born, let alone before you began to suffer. In our pain and prosperity alike, God fulfills His promises. His goodness demands that even when we do not understand how His redeeming work could possibly be executed in our lives, we ought to hope, and we will not be put to shame for doing so. In our lack of understanding we must cry out as Job did when his faith was strong, "Though He slay me, I will hope in Him". His love comes to us even through the pain we endure. His intention in all of what the enemy would work for evil, is for our good.

Who are we to call God to account? Who are we to claim that He has dealt unfairly with us? Alternatively, who are we to suppose that through our error we can overcome the sacrifice of Christ and drive God away from us?

We all may wrestle with anger in thinking that God has dealt with us unjustly. A pessimist may feel that God is a cruel master who refuses to bless those who obey and wounds them instead or disregards them entirely. A pessimistic believer may despair in the midst of their sins believing that God will withhold love from them for their errors. Yet, when Elihu comes to Job as his friend and rebukes him, he puts both of these mentalities to the test.

Firstly he poses the question, "When you sin, what have you done to Him?".

Not a thing! Your sin harms you and those around you, it is offensive to the nature of God, but you do not harm *Him*. Even the suffering and murder of His Son Jesus Christ for the forgiveness of sins was Christ subjecting Himself of His own accord as a sacrificial lamb. As it has been said, "You contribute nothing to your salvation except the sin that made it necessary"[20]. However, make no mistake that the cross was not something we inflicted upon Christ but it was an affliction that He chose on our behalf. It was by God's own choice, design, and desire that He was crucified for our salvation. None could have taken His life, but He laid it down.

You can flee from Him, rebel against Him, incur natural and supernatural consequences in your life as results of your sin, but the cry of a repentant heart pleads the blood of Christ over our lives and like the walls of Jericho

---

[20] Variously attributed to Jonathan Edwards, Martin Luther, and Philip Melancthon

every barrier between us and God collapses in a heap. Sin may have cornered you and made you feel separate from God, but repentance is the key which swings the door wide, where we can walk in the light of His presence again. If we feel the withdrawal of God's presence in our lives while we are caught in our sins, it is not to punish us, but to draw us near to Him again. God is not petty or passive aggressive. He does not hold His love hostage from you. If you feel the sting of sin in your life, turn to God and you will find Him there.

Elihu immediately follows this question up with the opposite angle. "If you are righteous, what do you give Him?" Again the answer is, not a thing!

We add nothing to God by way of our righteous living. God receives nothing from us other than what He has already been owed. By definition, living righteously means to live rightly. In other words, it means to live as we ought to. God will never owe us anything for us giving our lives to Him. Even if Christ had never come to our rescue, He would still deserve every moment, every thought, and every deed in your life.

In Job 34: 14-15 we see, "If God were to bring back the breath He has given *all* flesh would perish". Our Heavenly Father created you and me for us to give Him our whole lives. All of our praise and all of our obedience. That is the purpose for which we have breath!

Everything we have in this world was given out of His generosity, and He has gone even further in maintaining the world and preventing it from falling to its full destruction under the influence of sinful man. Again He extends His generous Spirit in sending Christ to redeem us to Himself. Again still, His Spirit blesses us by awakening our souls to know Him and to draw close to the fount of all life!

Even if we were to faithfully give every moment of our days in flawless love and obedience we will only have finally succeeded in doing what we ought to have done all along.

This idea is deeply repugnant to our human nature, and in a modern culture which has been heavily influenced by the humanist and the hedonist it can be very challenging to shake this repulsion. Unfortunately, we frequently take on a warped view of God until we understand our relationship with Him to have some kind of exchange rate. One in which we can deposit righteous living and store up blessings for ourselves. No wonder when troubles come, instead of people responding by running to God for shelter, we turn to Him with disappointment which gives way to bitterness and often leads us into pessimism.

Look instead at eternity. God has cleared a path to eternal life in perfect communion with Him. A life which will never be marred by pain or loss. Where we will be filled with everlasting joy, unwavering peace, and all of this has been purchased on your behalf. Not only does He provide the eternal reward, as well as the means which makes it possible, He has sent His Spirit as our Great helper who awakens our souls to lay hold of this treasure and to enter our rest without letting go of it. Those who follow the Lord in the present age are marked by love, joy, peace, patience, kindness, generosity, faithfulness, gentleness and self-control[21]. Each of these being the mark of someone who loves Jesus, obeys His commandments, and has seen the Spirit of God work inside of them. Likewise, each of these fruits is a blessing to our lives on the micro and macro scale.

Only when we realize that we add nothing to God by our righteousness, and in fact we are the beneficiaries of living according to His Word, will we find ourselves hard-pressed to take up offense against Him for the crime of unmet expectations.

Thankfully, God loved Job, and God loves us, too much to permit him to remain in error. Also, it is worth noting that while God does issue a rebuke, first by way of Elihu and secondly by His own Word, this is not a spiteful lashing out at Job. His rebuke is firm and authoritative, but as Scripture tells us, "He disciplines the one whom He loves"[22]. Job is met at the height of his entitled negativity with a *loving rebuke* from a friend and a God who desires his good.

A beautiful example of God's sovereignty can be seen in this friend's name, which we have already mentioned a few times.

---

[21] Galatians 5:22-23
[22] Hebrews 12:6 and Proverbs 3:12

"Elihu", meaning "My God is He".

This name sets the tone for the entirety of Elihu's rebuke. Rather than calling to mind Job's circumstances, or past, or conduct, he repeatedly declares the nature of God in the face of Job's suffering and despairing. This is how we ought to destroy our pessimism. With the truth of who God is. In Job 36:26 Elihu delivers a mighty blow to the accuser's position. One which should convict us all if we find ourselves questioning God in light of our distress, and wondering if He has failed or abandoned us.

"Behold, God is great, and we know Him not,"

Every day, the greatness of God is manifested in front of our very eyes. Every breath that comes into our lungs and oxygenates the blood which helps our organs maintain their myriad functions is given to us by God, and Scripture goes so far as to tell us that it is His very own breath which is given to us. Every creature from the smallest to the greatest exists and thrives within His perfectly balanced universe which has been masterfully calibrated for life to flourish. From the stars burning with unquenchable fire over centuries in the vacuum of space, to the rain drop which descends to the parched Earth below, we see in everything God is mighty and He is benevolent.

Yet we *know* Him not.

We see God's feats, and we watch the outworkings of His power and nature, but still we do not *know* Him in any comprehensive sense. Never could we imagine wrapping our minds around Him or His will. We can know God relationally, we can know God experimentally, but we can never know God comprehensively or completely. Even what He has revealed to us of His nature and will, is explained as though to little children.

Even so, this does not stop many pessimists from counting on their understanding when they attempt to contradict the nature of God. You see, as humans we can fall into a trap of building our understanding up as the authority for how our expectations should be fulfilled. We absolutely should trust and expect that God will fulfill His promises! He is a good and faithful God whose Word shall not return void. It's when we attempt to hold Him accountable to our expectations of *how* those promises will be fulfilled that we are fashioning a god after our own likeness and have mistaken personal demand for faith-filled expectation. So, when the hand of God does not move in harmony with our demands, we judge Him instead of the imitation of Him that has been sculpted to our liking.

We cannot hope to approach comprehending the scope or nuance of God's majestic plan. How can we hope to understand why He involves Himself in the lifecycle of a flower which blooms in a field one day and is gone the next? Why does His power and majesty condescend to our humble planet to clothe that lily in glorious splendor only for it to fade without ever being seen? How much more are we perplexed by how it serves to glorify Him, and work out the continuous perfecting of all life unto Christ's return? Do we presume to dictate to Him how He should repay our righteousness? Or how He ought to fulfill His promises to us? Or how He ought to display His nature and power in our lives?

We do not *know* Him, nor could we ever hope to comprehend His ways.

Occasionally this results in our thinking that we are utterly forsaken or alone, as Job did in his flagging faith. We find him crying out in his accusation against the Father that he does not see the hand of the Almighty at work. In light of our minute understanding and God's incomprehensible will, we can be honest here and admit that we often find ourselves unable to discern His works. Job 35:13-16 has a powerful and convicting reply to our doubts in such moments.

"...God does not heed an empty cry...How much less when you say that you do not see Him."

It is a profound foolishness to mistake our not seeing the hand of God at work as proof that He is absent. Who are we that our understanding has become the standard by which God's holiness is measured? What qualifies us to take inventory of our lives and call God to account for where we find what we perceive to be a discrepancy in the fulfillment of His promises? Can our suffering disprove the revealed nature of God? Never! God has not once been absent or cruel in our suffering. His love, goodness, kindness, and righteousness are present and flawlessly at work even *through* our deepest agony. There is no pit of sorrow so deep that we can be removed from God's presence, purpose, or power.

Pessimism accepts as truth that everything has a bend towards negative outcomes which compound into progressively worsening results, and it is by luck or sheer willpower that anything ends favorably in this life. Not only that, but anything that *does* go well will ultimately and rapidly fall apart. The pessimist Christian is forced by such beliefs to strip their hope in salvation of all its riches until salvation from Hell and the second coming of Christ may be all that remains to give light to them in the valley. Heaven and eternal rest do wait for us, and at times that may very well be all that we have to cling to in the storms of life. However, it should not be all the Hope we try to gather, and it is certainly not all that we have been offered. We are offered heavenly treasures, not just at the end of our lives, but even now. Chief among these promises, we have access to and communion with the God of the universe.

Perhaps your life has wrung the joy and hope out of you like a dishrag. Maybe you never had the opportunity to lay hold of it in the first place.

Whatever the case may be, I want to take a moment now to impart to you the words of Jehovah in response to Job's complaint. This is our reminder of who God has revealed Himself to be, and hopefully we can turn our eyes upon Him so that all the things of this world will grow dim. Let us give Him our attention and see how trusting His truth radically transforms how we look at the facts which fill our lives. I recommend reading along with Job 38 during this next portion of the book. Also, I ask that you allow your imagination to stretch and get carried away by the imagery used by God. He gave us imaginations for a reason, and I believe all too often we are afraid to use them in religious matters for fear of error. Here though we can be confident as it is God Himself leading us by the hand.

God speaks to Job from the midst of the whirlwind. A force which is a physical embodiment of chaos and destruction. Here we find that God's design and divine order are sovereign even over the crazed winds. Though to our eyes the wind follows no discernable course, every gust has been measured and directed according to His purpose.

He alone laid the foundations of the Earth. He set the cornerstone on which the entire planet was built. Consider, this may be the Earth's core, and may even predate the creation narrative! Scripture tells us that the Earth was shapeless and void, so it was already present only needing to be shaped to His design and filled with His creative work. Therefore, this foundation reaches even beyond the knowledge which God has given to us. God alone possesses the blueprints of the world; having full knowledge of the precise dimensions to which He fashioned it. Our world was not merely thrown together, but was intimately tailored by the Father's hands. Like a skilled craftsman building a mansion for his children, God has lovingly overseen and personally placed every detail. From sweeping shorelines to the nectar of a honeysuckle. In stark contrast, even in our modern age we do not *know for certain* what the Earth is built on. Even with all our scientific advancement we can only hope to hazard an educated guess at what it is that God chose for its foundation.

In Job 38:7 we are told that during the laying of the Earth's cornerstone there was a celebration in the Heavens. God was beginning the work of our creation, and there was a pre-Earth creation which sang with rejoicing over His workmanship, long before we ever drew a breath!

When the seas were birthed into existence (again part of the pre-creation narrative as the Holy Spirit hovered above the waters 3.6) God was the one who brought forth its billowing waves. He set its boundaries with the chains of gravity, the walls of shores, the weights of atmospheric pressure. Then He blanketed clouds over the seas and wrapped space around our planet. How beautiful is this imagery, of God enclosing our atmosphere in the swaddling cloths of the universe.

Every day of our lives the Lord has drawn up the sun over the horizon from night into morning. It rises not by our will or influence, but by the intentional action of God.

Very fitting for our day and age, we see that *all justice comes by His hand*. The *only* reason wickedness falters and justice ever prevails is due to our Holy God working in our fallen world.

He has traveled the hidden deep places to which man will never venture. He walks as easily in these impossible places as He did in the Garden of Eden when the world was new. Not only does He journey in these secret places, but He comprehends them in their entirety while we must strain our imaginations even to wrestle with their existence.

Light, darkness, every element, provision, even life and death obey the will of the Almighty God.

He sends the healing rains and the blistering winds. When the ground has cried out for life-giving waters, He has heard and knows the very seed which lays scattered in the dirt that receives the rain. When the darkened thunderclouds stampede from their heavenly stables in terrible fury, and blanket the skies, He holds them by the reins and directs them to where they go. In even living and dying, fruitfulness and destruction, He fulfills His promises and works a good that is often beyond our perception and *always* beyond our understanding. Even the constellations themselves have been tethered in space by His hand.

So, when terror befalls you, and you feel as though you are cast out to sea, how do you keep from burdening yourself further with the sin of despair?

We must set our focus on the truth. That God truly is all-powerful and reigns above every natural or supernatural authority. Simultaneously He is intimately and personally responsible for the rhythm of the entire universe. Even still, all of this is only made good news to us by the truth that God is also entirely good. When tragedy comes into our life we can trust in the truth over the circumstances, and follow a pattern of thinking that is built on these foundational truths of God's nature. Nothing can come to me except by my Father's hands, and He is for me not against me. I can trust that God is redeeming and will redeem all things for good, not just my good, but the good of all who follow Him.

If all of this is true, then pessimism is a trait of the old flesh. It deserves to be cast aside as the insidious enemy it is. It poisons the streams of living water in our hearts, and if we water our hearts with this tainted brew, we will bear sickly fruit. Pessimism spoils the fruits of the Spirit in our lives and bows the branches of our hearts with worry that we are not meant to carry.

Proverbs tells us to watch after the streams of our heart 3.7. As landowners likely know, when you have a stream on your property it is necessary to survey it upstream to ensure that there are no blockages, or worse still rotting animal carcasses in the water. Why is this? Because any water downstream of the rotting animal will be poisoned by its presence. This affects the irrigation of everything downstream which draws its life from those polluted waters. So then, pessimists, plead with the Spirit to walk with you and search your heart, as David did[23]. Listen to Him when He shines His light on these rotting disappointments, idols, and pride which have polluted His blessings to you. And with the Spirit, heave them up out of the waters and burn them on the shore-side so that you may be free of them, and drink of the pure streams of living water.

When trouble comes, call to mind Job's friend Elihu. He asked Job questions which his own name answered for us. These things are written for our benefit, and I believe we would be good to use them as grounding safeguards against despair.

Who is the Almighty author of all creation?

My God is He!

Who loves me as His precious child?

My God is He!

---

[23] Psalm 139:23-24

Who guards me, and allows nothing to pass which will not be redeemed for my eternal good?

My God is He!

How can I possibly muster despair within me if this is who my God is? Hope naturally springs forth because it is born of unassailable truth which stretches in all directions throughout eternity. God's unchanging nature is the rock beneath our feet, even when the raging storms of life obscure our vision and batter our bodies. If our knees buckle, if we are thrown face down, we will not be cast headlong into disaster because we land on the rock which we are standing on!

Because we know the light of God cannot be doused. His will for us is unstained by fear, doubt, or wicked intention. His hand cannot be turned back by all the force of every enemy in the heavens or on Earth or below the Earth. He sits on the throne above every throne, He is the King of kings, and the Lord of lords. He is the Uncreated One. He is the one who condescended to Earth, lived, died, and rose again so that my eternal salvation is secured. He sits on the mercy seat of Heaven. My name is written on His heart. He is the Alpha and Omega whose Kingdom will come and He will kill death and place all evil under lock and key, and will walk with us in the eternal day as we have perfect communion with Him. His

Kingdom is here now and is coming. He has given us life more abundantly.

Have hope. Do not despair.

My God is He.

Chapter 4

Worshipping in the Prison: Optimism

Before we begin to evaluate the Biblical shortcomings of optimism, I want to reiterate that I was once an optimist. For most of my life I believed that not only was optimism preferable, it was also Biblically mandated. This whole book began as my attempt to argue my case for optimism. What I found instead was that while I do believe a positive outlook is an admirable attribute of optimism, the worldview itself is weak and Biblically unsound. It is the hollow mimicry of Biblical hope, and ultimately the optimist is no better off than the pessimist.

Both can be led into sin and gross error by their preferred outlooks. Both worldviews are rooted in skewed views of self, life, and God's nature. Whereas pessimism is infuriatingly stubborn as facts upon facts seem to pile up with ample supporting evidence, optimism is inherently fragile and passionately shielded by those who live by it. Optimism is largely dependent on misplaced values and interpretations of God's promises. In the hardest of times, it cannot stare wickedness, pain, and loss in the face, let alone overcome them. It must always be shielded and kept in conscious quarantine from direct opposition.

One of the primary shortcomings of optimism is that when it is pressed to its limits by difficult circumstances, it breeds willfully ignorant people. Frequently, optimists must resign themselves to a "preferable submission" in order to preserve their cheerful disposition. A preferable submission being the moment when one is forced to either succumb to despair or to remain positive despite all evidence and motivation to the contrary. An optimist will typically choose the more comfortable of two unsavory options. When left with two options which will ultimately not affect the outcome, the optimist decides that cheerful ignorance is better than despairing acceptance. Herein lies the most fundamental difference between optimism and hope. Optimism has to be protected *by us*, while Biblical hope supplies protection *for us*.

Our Biblical text for this chapter is a well-known passage which gives us a prime example of positivity in action within a godly framework. This passage gives us a practical view of a hope which is more durable than optimism, even in the face of severe hardship. We will be looking at the story of Paul and Silas worshiping in the prison as well as the verses immediately preceding. The story also offers us a look at an unflattering form of optimism, and the contrast that arises when placed side by side with the hope of the prisoners is stark.

Acts 16 presents us with Paul and Silas as strangers in a foreign land. In all likelihood they would have been in high spirits as they searched for a place of worship to minister and pray. Lydia had just come to the faith in a beautiful testimony of the Spirit's faithfulness[24]. Previous passages tell us

---

[24] Acts 16:11-40

that even though Lydia was a Gentile, she possessed knowledge from divine revelation that Jehovah was the true and living God. Because of this, she recognized God's truth in the preaching of Paul and Silas, and the Spirit moved on her to bring the truth to bear on her life. Though she was a woman of wealth and influence, she did not hesitate to count it all as lost and submit herself to the Lordship of her Heavenly Father.

This context is vitally important to the beginning of this passage, because it shows us the way Christ deals with His bride in contrast to the way our enemy deals with his prey. All Lydia did was worship and obey, and God blessed her with revelation which had been concealed by Him since before the foundations of the Earth[25]. He made Himself known to her so closely, that she was able to recognize the truth of the Gospel immediately and lay everything at the feet of Jesus in reply.

Once this story begins in earnest and brings us across the path of the wicked men, we see what steep price the enemy demands for even a shadow of divine knowledge. These men did not concern themselves with the ancient secrets of the Most High God, and neither did their clientele. Customers were able to fork over their payment and look into the eyes of the demon tormented girl in chains, who was twice a slave in spirit and body, and receive insight into the trivial and temporal matters of their lives.

---

[25] Matthew 13:35

Lydia was blessed and rejoiced in her blessing. Even though it did not bring her any physical comfort or financial gain, and in fact she had plenty of each which was put at significant risk in submitting to the Lord. Her hope went further than physical comforts. Conversely, we see the girl who was bound by an unclean spirit of divination. How cruel a beast that it did not take a man who could rule with influence granted by its knowledge, but a child who could be easily exploited by others. In this way it not only robbed a child of her freedom and life, but it had also thrown her as fuel onto the fire of greed in the hearts of her masters. In submission Lydia laid hold of an eternal and unfailing hope which could never be taken from her, no matter what ruin may come to her as a consequence. For all their exploitation and wickedness these men had only managed to store up for themselves what could vanish in an instant.

The way optimists respond to God, unfortunately, tends to have less in common with Lydia and a great deal more in common with the masters of the demon possessed girl. Far from humility and counting all we have as forfeit, we instead fall into outrage, not realizing that it is motivated by the belief that God's power is given to lift us out of our circumstances rather than redeem them for our good. There is the assumption in modern America especially that "our good" is synonymous with "our comfort". However, we must realize that our comfort may not actually be to our good or to the good of others! After all, how can we hope to genuinely minister of the depths of God's love and sufficiency when we have only ever needed to wade ankle deep into it? Just as Paul ultimately kicked the crutch out from beneath these wicked men, do not suppose that God will not allow or even *do the same to you*, so that you will be forced to learn to walk with Him.

Returning to the story of Acts 16, the slave girl followed Paul and Silas around town for "several days". Each day, as they worked to minister to those in need, they were bombarded by her screams and crying out. She shrieked and cried that these men were proclaiming the way of salvation.

Both men were foreigners in a strange land. A land which did not value nor broadly believe in the God of Israel. They were tasked with the difficult work of bringing the light of the Lord into a community that was not only ignorant of the Gospel, but into a place which was hostile towards God's reign. Their audience had become comfortable with counterfeit blessings, and God's common graces. Her harassment was nothing compared to the public unrest which may occur if they were to rebuke her or perhaps even deal more severely with her. They were far from any safety net they may have enjoyed in a more familiar city and were already tasked with delicate work treating the heart of the issue rather than the symptom.

Eventually though, Paul had enough. Many days of her hindering their efforts had rid him of any further concern with tact or propriety.

God is patient with the immature believer who clings to the crutch of optimism. He is often willing to endure our fragile and incomplete views of His hope for a season, but make no mistake, He desires greater riches for you and me. We cannot think that we may go around proclaiming that Christ preaches the way of salvation and expect that there will not be a moment when He turns to us and dashes our current state of mind, knocking off the chains we wear and freeing the Gospel from the hindrances we have placed on it in our own hearts. God brings about great spiritual maturation in us when our understanding is confronted with His revelation. When we learn that God is so much greater, and wholly other, than what we supposed Him to be.

A danger posed by the mock hope of optimism is that our positive outlook births expectations which become the face of God to us. So, when those expectations are not met, and are utterly destroyed beyond our ability to rationalize to our "hope" we believe that God has failed us, and we despair. Whereas when we hope in God to do what is right and what is for our good as Scripture describes them, we will always be able to trace our unmet expectations back to our own flawed understanding. Again, we see the similarity between optimism and pessimism, and we see the contrast with Biblical hope. With Biblical hope, God is the constant by which everything else is measured against. Therefore, hope can withstand disappointment when optimism either works desperately to ignore/diminish it, or it breaks and throws the heartache in the face of God, in disgust.

God loves us too much to allow us to remain unopposed in our error. This is why Proverbs tells us that He disciplines the one whom He loves. He has made the immeasurable riches of His glory available to us by our baptism into new life! Why would he permit us to be satisfied with cozy theology which cannot save, fruitless theology which does not reproduce salvation in others, or misled theology in which we praise a bespoke version of God.

When Paul at last sets the girl free from her spiritual bondage, her physical chains were likewise loosened. Yet even God acting in spectacular fashion to release her from her misery had no favorable effect on her masters. There was no conviction in their hearts over their wickedness and their systems of extortion. They found no problem with having turned a blind eye to the evil roots of their good fortune and security. Where was their blame and fury cast if not onto their own actions? Their spite was cast upon God and on His people once freedom and justice were given to the girl at the expense of their comfort.

Have you considered that the goodness of God towards you and towards others may be to the detriment of your comfort, goals, or priorities?

When God enters into your life circumstances in power and fulfills His promises, not by removing the trials but by bringing you *through* them, is your worldview shaken? If in doing the work of the Kingdom, you find yourself thrown in jail instead of receiving good health and material prosperity, will you still believe in an all powerful and all good Heavenly Father? Or will you feel as though He has failed or deceived you? If I tell you that God may call you, His beloved child, to live penniless, imprisoned, and/or plagued by illness for the sake of the Gospel would it steal the hallelujah off your lips?

Hopefully, now some of the similarities I mentioned before concerning optimism and pessimism are becoming clearer. Both are grounded in twisted views of God which leave us open to the lure of abandoning the truth we have received. Perhaps if we are honest with ourselves we will find that optimism threatens to lead us into worshiping idols rather than worshiping God. Look at some of our American Church's evangelism tactics in this light and the evidence becomes clear. We tell children that life without Jesus is hard, and that following Jesus is the better way to live, without ever defining what a better way to live looks like in light of Scripture rather than culture. We tell fellow believers, much like Job's friends told him, that the reason their life may be hard is because they are not following Jesus well enough.

Having grown up in church my whole life I have been on the receiving end and the giving end of some of these faulty strategies. In reality, even if we were capable of following Jesus perfectly we can still "lose at life". Do not work to convince yourself or others that the carnal self will find the righteous path preferable. The road is narrow and difficult and beset on all sides with enemies that seek your destruction! You can gather all these material treasures to yourself in far easier and more effective ways than by living for Jesus.

Our comfort is of lesser concern to God than salvation. Even comfort in the hands of a faithful Christian is first and foremost a tool which God uses to further His eternal kingdom. Go to the gamblers, the dealers, the enslavers, and the thieves if you want to hoard wealth, ease, and comfort. God has concerned Himself with the winning of souls, and He was willing to put His only begotten Son to death in order to do so! Will He not do likewise with those adopted in His name? Do not suppose that Jesus came to remove us from difficulty in this life. He came so that even though the battle may rage all around us we will have peace and hope because our victory is sure.

There are those, especially in modern times, who have hacked away at, twisted, and diluted Scripture in order to affirm their god of comfort. For the sake of more thoroughly addressing the flaws in this optimist mentality, I would like to touch on a passage often used to fit their purposes.

"The thief comes only to steal and kill and destroy. I came that they may have life and have it abundantly"
John 10:10 (ESV)

Why is it that so many seem to interpret this promise from Jesus to be proof positive that His followers will experience less hardship, less struggle, or less pain? A prevailing belief seems to be that what Jesus is promising is either a removal *of* or a removal *from* our negative circumstances. Of course, this sounds wonderful to hurting hearts! Who wouldn't want to follow a Jesus who will relieve every financial and personal burden? Masses of hurting people flock to churches which say that Jesus wants to give us abundant life but in actuality they are preaching that He gives us *easier* life.

A Christian optimist recites extra-Biblical and unbiblical phrases such as, "Jesus wouldn't give you more than you can bear" or "It's never as bad as it seems" and "It is going to get better, because God is working all things together for your good". What do we do with faithful believers whose circumstances never do "get better"? Why do we suppose that since God is capable of removing our hardships then He *must* remove them in order to be good? This is a fundamental argument of many atheists, that if God is all powerful then He is not all good because of the suffering present in creation.

Optimism places a Christian veneer over this idea and calls it prosperity theology. It dictates the standards by which God's goodness and power can be validated. It expects that God will elevate us out of trouble or remove the trouble for us. But this is not life abundant! More abundantly means an adding to, it means something that is over and beyond the present state. A theology of God removing every obstacle and relieving every struggle is not a Gospel of abundance, but a Gospel of reduction. The clear and obvious danger of such a gospel is that in an eventuality where God in His own wise counsel deems it best for us to tarry a little while in our trials it can be devastating to our entire belief system. Optimism is a hope for gain, but with our eyes on the wrong prize. Is not the treasure God has stored up for us in Heaven better than anything we could ever ask for or imagine?[26] Why do we expect that the gain God has promised will reflect what our own carnal desires can conjure?

When all those structures and idols we look to are cast down or stripped away from us, optimism ultimately leaves us in the same place as the masters of the demon possessed slave girl. They had lived in relative ease and wealth, satisfied with a perverse glimpse of divine knowledge so long as it propped up their lifestyle. Then God issued His servant to bring it crashing down around their ears. Paul did what was right and just, at great risk to himself, and causing significant harm to the life that these men had cherished. The destruction of their way of life was for the good of the girl who gained her spiritual liberation, the good of any onlookers as they saw the powerful works of the Spirit, the good of Paul and Silas as they lived in obedience to their Lord, the good of us to hear and know the Lord's nature and power, and the good of the men themselves that they could no longer practice the cancerous sin which had furnished their wants for so long. Still they cursed God and attacked His servants.

---

[26] Ephesians 3:20

This is where we see the contrast in how Paul and Silas respond to a tangible and painful trial.

After they had been seized, shamed, beaten, and thrown into the deepest darkest hole in the prison, unsure if they would ever see the light of day again, they prayed and sang hymns to God. Certainly, they prayed to God for their release. Maybe they prayed for the girl as she had been set free from her spiritual bondage, and maybe they even prayed for the men whose rage had placed them there. Perhaps they prayed for wisdom and discernment in how to conduct themselves if they were faced with an authority figure to whom they could plead their case. These were men after all, not angels or deities, they were men in anguish. Surely, they wept bitterly and fought with their battered flesh as it no doubt bade them to "curse God and die". Yet their hope did not crumble. It did not require there to be an absence of peril so that it could be preserved. Their view of God and relationship with Him formed their reality rather than the other way around.

God has promised us peace that surpasses all understanding, not peace that surpasses all reason. It is a peace that seems nonsensical to those who have not tasted and seen that the Lord is good, and instead are left with only what they understand; that is their circumstances in carnal knowledge. But this hope is nonetheless reasonable once seen in the light of God's glory.

It is this peace which invaded that pitch black prison cell and the Spirit of God breathed joy, peace, faith, and hope into the bruised and broken bodies of His servants. There was no sense or reason to try to encourage one another with flimsy platitudes about silver linings and that God would never give them more than they could bear. They had been given a heavy load to shoulder. However, they did not surrender to despair and protest against God's design. Rather in the midst of their pain and terror, their hope lifted them up to praise and cry aloud and worship God! Not because they saw His hand at work, not because they saw a clear escape from their trials, but because they *knew God's nature* and trusted Him. So, they could confidently exalt His name and rejoice in Him in the midst of their ordeal.

This is what life more abundantly looks like. Life which cannot be overcome by death or destruction. It cannot be stolen by villains, it weathers every storm, and thrives in the wasteland.

As I studied this concept of hope versus optimism, and specifically life more abundantly, God brought to mind a fitting example that can be found in the natural world. In the North American deserts there is a plant called the Great Saguaro Cactus. This prickly plant manages to grow in the midst of a tortuous environment. There is scorching heat, little water, and little reason for, need for, or aid to the life of a Saguaro Cactus. Yet these stubborn cacti grow to massive heights of 30-40 feet above the sandy desert floor! Not only that, but they defy the elements which constantly work to destroy them by frequently living to be over 100 years old.

One might think that this is where the illustration would end. That may be a lovely testament to the perseverance of the Christian, and their ability from the Spirit to survive the hardest of times, but as we have mentioned I do not believe that is the extent of God's promises to us. That would be life, stubborn and enduring, but it would not necessarily be life *abundantly*.

We see in Job's rebuke that God is responsible for the plants which spring to life all over our globe. Even those which sprout up for but a moment in the cosmic march of time, lending no shade to any creature and being seen by no man or woman before ultimately withering away with the world seemingly unchanged by its presence. God is intimately, directly, and purposefully involved in every moment of that plant's existence. So it is that God directs each moment of our lives, and the life of the Saguaro Cactus. It is God who sets it up in protest against the harshest elements. All the more miraculously, it is God who causes it to bloom and bear fruit.

He does not remove the cactus from the desert. Instead, He brings it to have life moreover in the midst of that which works tirelessly to kill and erase it from the face of the Earth. Biblical Hope is not merely a coping mechanism helping us survive. That is the goal of optimism, surviving. Avoiding or seeking to control any hardship which may afflict us.

Hope, however, is modeled by Paula and Silas as they hung from their shackles in the dungeon. God's mission had led them there. With intention and attention, He had planted these men in the desert surrounded by a context which consistently sought their destruction. Yet these men did more than endure. They also did not withdraw or flee from the hardships which faithfulness to God would bring. Paul after-all could have sent the girl away, keeping the peace with the locals while also removing the impediment to his ministry. Instead, he had liberated her, and traded his freedom for hers.

There was no avoidance, and the worship of the two men was not a manner of seeking control over their hardships. Worship by its nature is contrary to control. It is an act of divine submission to something beyond yourself. Whereas the slave owners raged against the loss of their comfort and apparent control, these prisoners further submitted themselves to the will of the Father who they knew was present even in their darkest hours.

What was the result? The power of the darkness, which kept them bound and subject to its oppressive control was utterly sundered. Freedom is found in hope! Had the walls remained sound, had the chains remained on their wrists, had they been led before a council of elders and murdered in the streets darkness and woe would still have had no power over their souls. I would argue that these men were free before the prison walls split. The physical manifestation of freedom was a reflection of the spiritual liberty they already possessed.

Again, enduring with life and freedom which cannot be extinguished by our circumstances or context is without a doubt one of the blessings of Biblical Hope. Yet we see that the beauty goes even beyond this blessing. Hope defends the bearer and brings freedom and life to others. Hope does not require our tireless guardianship to flourish or survive. It is not a fickle rose of the soul which withers if the soil is rocky or dry or even the least bit less than entirely hospitable.

Paul and Silas possessed hope which secured them, freed them, and even produced new life in those around them.

This is what life more abundantly looks like when faced with terrible perils and agony. It looks like blooming in the desert. It looks like singing in the prison. Life abundantly looks like the jailer and his household coming to faith by the grace and power displayed to him by his charges. Hope breathes life into failing limbs; it sets us against our foes and keeps us upright, and gives us the strength to bring others into freedom and new life as well.

Chapter 5

Redeeming Pain for Purity: Why hope when we suffer?

Now that we have taken a look at both Optimism and Pessimism and where they fall short, I want to cover instances where we experience crises of faith, and how Biblical Hope can be a present help in our time of need. None of the chapters are comprehensive by any means, but they do provide practical strategies for our life struggles. We will begin with Hope when we suffer. The suffering we will be focusing on here is "external suffering". Suffering that we are afflicted with by outside forces rather than suffering that we inflict upon ourselves as consequences of sinful choices.

Until the second coming of Christ, suffering is woven into the human condition as a consequence of sin in our world. This may not seem very encouraging, but it is important to acknowledge the reality in which we live as humans in a broken world which is desperately groaning for the finishing of God's redemptive work. For us to glorify God fully, and for us to understand Him and grow close to Him in any way that will actually bear fruit we must not shrink away from the facts of life. As we just finished covering, this is a method of thinking which starves and weakens our faith. Neither can we stop short of introducing the truth of the Gospel of Jesus Christ into the circumstances, which is where we find our hope. Through Him, even the suffering of the world will be and is being redeemed. Christ Himself was called a "man of sorrows".[27] In His life He became intimately

---

[27] Isaiah 53:3

acquainted with suffering and torment which no man, woman, or child throughout all of history can claim comparison.

Because of the immeasurable heights of glory which He enjoyed and set aside for our sake, the depths of despair to which He allowed Himself to descend are so great that we could never truly empathize with Him. This does mean that though we cannot empathize with His suffering, because of the depth of His affliction we can never go beyond the reach of His empathy and compassion towards us.

Due to both Christ's death and His resurrection, we find in 1 Peter 1:3-7 that we have received, in the midst of our circumstances and suffering, a steadfast *living* hope. Our hope is not found in that we should be exempt from suffering in this world. In fact, if that were the claim of Christianity then it would have failed miserably. When the hope in our Savior is pitched as rescue from the burden of today, the security of our faith is made reliant on our circumstances rather than the sufficient work of Jesus. Believing that Christ promises us health, wealth, and comfort is cheapening the Gospel rather than laying hold of it. In so doing we manage to hamstring our faith and shackle ourselves to the rotting corpse of the old flesh and its desires, which is supposed to be cast aside at our rebirth in Christ.[28]

The reality of our hope in Christ is specific and strong. It is specific in that there is no room allowed by Scripture for us to reinterpret or retrofit the Gospel in order to make it more palatable or to help us *feel* as though it is

---

[28] Ephesians 4:22

more applicable or useful to us. God has graciously provided instruction so that we would not be left to wonder about the scope and nature of our salvation. It is also *strong*. Not just strong as a singular event which remains steadfast albeit static and lifeless. Praise God that we have a *living* hope! By the resurrection of Christ who will never die, we too have a hope which will never expire. The eternally living Son of God is the collateral which our hope can borrow against, and which our suffering can never exhaust. More beautiful still, a living hope can come to *you*. A living hope does not only act as a bulwark which you can hide behind, but it can also rise and fight for you as the Great Defender. It cannot be circumvented, bypassed, overcome, or outwitted because our living hope is Christ Himself. He has secured an imperishable inheritance for us. Purchased and released to us by His death. Secured and galvanized against all trouble, condemnation, and circumstance by His resurrection. This hope is strong enough to endure any depression, job loss, illness, agony, or even the severest suffering one can imagine.

The suffering of a regenerate believer should ultimately always culminate in worship. We are equipped to rejoice because His eternal promises will outlast any pain we may endure. His Holy Spirit, who gives us divine faith, places a steely resolve in the hearts of His children so that we may withstand the weight of the suffering we are subjected to. Like a tower which may groan and creak under an unbelievable weight and yet remain strong, we will not crumble beneath it because of the inner substance which upholds us. The Holy Spirit in power through faith girds our hearts like steel beams support the tower which is built around them. We can place our faith on Him and confidently step into that uncomfortable place of dependency. Because, despite our circumstances, God's goodness will forever remain unaltered, and His closeness will forever remain unchanged. If the ground itself were to rise and pitch like the waves on the sea, and all the oceans were to become as still as glass in defiance of nature's order, God's nature would remain eternally constant. Such a beautiful and potent truth is the key to how the Spirit can lovingly and justly keep the lantern of our faith burning even in our darkest hours.

God would have to be despicably cruel if He were to prop up a saint under the weight of their sorrows with no genuine or worthwhile relief and reward waiting for them on the other side of it all. How wicked a God would He be if He uplifted and sustained His children under every affliction that befell them without ransoming them into sweet, tender, and total salvation? As though the span of a man's life was to worship a God who sees him as some kind of praise battery which He can expend and dispose of. Such a Lord would be like the pagan gods found in mythologies the world over. There is no love, no Fatherly affection, no righteous Kingliness to such a God. All the same, such a view of God seems widely held by those who wish to justify their rebellion and disbelief. The accusation is well-worn, and I am sure any Christian who has had to make defense for their faith has heard it. That if there is a God, He is cruel, and callously allows His creation to suffer while selfishly demanding praise and devotion.

The God of *Scripture* is very different from this humanistic view. We see there that God created man and woman in a perfect relationship with Himself, with the design that they would grow and mature into increasingly deeper and more beautiful fellowship with their Creator. Humanity was created by nature to forever press further into the depths of the unsearchable God, and experience the joyous fulfillment of knowing, discovering, and experiencing the infinite, invisible, and incomprehensible Jehovah God!

Moreover, in the very *moment* when the curse of sin fractured the purity of God's perfect design, He promised our coming Savior and our assured salvation.[29] The very first messianic prophecy, a promise concerning Jesus, was issued by the Lord Himself in the same garden where He had been betrayed and rebelled against by His creation. God's promised salvation, while issued at the fall of man, has been established and unchanged since before the Earth was formless and void. Faith in this promised salvation is more precious than the finest gold. The purest gold can yet perish even though it has been purified by the hottest fires. There are forces in this world that test us far greater than even the hottest fires, and any Earthly purity will not be able to withstand it. But that which has been born in us of the Spirit cannot only endure these fires, but is only more *fully revealed* by

---

[29] Genesis 3:15

our trials.

Even if we are grieved by trials all our life long, it will not be because a cruel God finds delight in our misery, or because a cold and distant God has forgotten His children. He *redeems* our pain for purification and our misery is repurposed for renewal. God does not desire that His children would suffer, but He *does* desire that many may come to salvation through Jesus Christ, and there are times where the suffering of the unregenerate drives them into His arms and the suffering of His saints displays His sustaining power to draw the lost to Himself. He desires that we may come to know Jesus more deeply and fellowship with the God of Creation more fully and perfectly. Instead of our suffering being evidence that God has withdrawn from us, we will find that when we cry out to Him in our distress He is closer than a brother and that in our desire for sanctuary we will press deeper into His arms than ever before. He becomes, in a genuine and experimental sense, our refuge and the Rock of Ages in which we can hide ourselves.

A God who permits His children to suffer for their good, while He upholds them to accomplish their good work, is a good Father whose will is not beholden to how we feel. Although it is not popular in our culture to say this, pain is not only unavoidable, but it is at times also entirely necessary. He can love us perfectly and do what is fully good without any external sources dictating to Him what good means. Because God is good, He cannot do anything which is not good. This is why God is the Rock which we build our house on and not the house itself. Because there are storms that He will not shelter us from, but He will give us the strength to endure. Everything that we build on Him and His unchanging nature will stand forever, even though the storm still rages against it.

"Blessed be the God and Father of our Lord Jesus Christ! According to his great mercy, he has caused us to be born again to a living hope through the resurrection of Jesus Christ from the dead, to an inheritance that is imperishable, undefiled, and unfading, kept in heaven for you, who by God's power are being guarded through faith for a salvation ready to be revealed in the last time. In this you rejoice, though now for a little while, if necessary, you have been grieved by various trials, so that the tested genuineness of your faith—more precious than gold that perishes though it is tested by fire—may be found to result in praise and glory and honor at the revelation of Jesus Christ."

1 Peter 1:3-7 (ESV)

It is important to note in this passage Peter is addressing a congregation, not an individual. Because this is the case, we must interpret the encouragement in that particular context. This means that our suffering is not *just personal*. My suffering is not just about me, and your suffering is not just about you. When we are able to look beyond the borders of our own life and attempt to see our suffering from the bird's eye macro scale it can serve to further uplift us in our times of trouble.

Ask yourself, which is objectively more important or valuable, 80+ years of relative comfort and prosperity, or a single eternal soul snatched from the teeth of Hell because of how Christ was magnified through your "light and momentary affliction...not worth comparing to the glory that awaits"? This is not an oversimplification of the matter; it really does come down to a question of worth. Do we value what God values so dearly? Then we will be able to trust that God is redeeming our pain for greater value than our comfort could ever afford us. Mountains of the finest gold cannot purchase a soul from Hell, but the testimony of a tried believer may just snatch them from the flames!

Suffering does not mean God is cruel, because He is not passive in light of our torment. He gives our suffering a purpose and He gives us an objective.

Purpose: To draw us closer to Him, and to make Him known.
Objective: To draw closer to Him, and to make Him known.

This is all the more confirmed by the wording of the Apostle. He cites that this suffering is for a "little while" and "is necessary". Our suffering has utility, but *it is temporary* because its usefulness is finite. Sorrow and suffering are not endless streams which can run on forever without ceasing. God's glory and our eternal well-being may at times be best displayed and furthered by momentary suffering, but it will not always be so. Our God who is fully good and fully just, free of flaw or error will not permit a moment of suffering beyond its usefulness. The Creator who has held the seasons in balance since the beginning of time will not err and allow you to experience a day of suffering outside of its fruitful season.

Our ability to endure is bolstered by the fact that our suffering is not some wildfire which rages out of control, mindlessly consuming everything in its path. At times it will feel as though this is the case. There is suffering in this world which is so beyond us in terms of power that we can feel certain that nothing will turn it aside and extinguish it before we are utterly destroyed by it. Honestly, there are times where we live and die in our suffering, not receiving our relief until the Lord rescues us eternally into His embrace forever.

Yet we can rejoice in steadfast hope, because though we may agonize in our suffering, by God's grace it is not for our ultimate destruction but for our ultimate good! God has divine and perfect intention which is worked through any suffering permitted to come our way. This gives us hope because it gives our suffering meaningfulness. Our trials are not mindless crimes we are subjected to and victimized by without purpose or meaning, but instead the hand of God redeems them all for the eternally meaningful mission of rescuing souls from Hell and drawing us closer to Him.

Coupling this powerful truth with the reminder that all of our suffering is temporary should serve to bolster the spirits of a weary believer. Suffering is part of life in our sinful and broken world. You may suffer all your life, but your suffering will not last forever if your name is written in the Lamb's Book of Life. When compared with everlasting eternity, time without end, forever and ever with our blessed Savior, all our years are a single breath by comparison. Look at your life even in the scope of history. Tens of thousands of years stretch out behind your 80 year or so life span. Yet even all of history that has happened and is yet to come is even *smaller* in comparison with eternity, and eternity is what awaits us!

Paul went so far as to say that this *light and momentary* affliction will not be worth comparing to the glory that awaits us in Heaven.[30] Let us think about this in the negative as well.

If all the agony, affliction, and trials of a life lived in service to the Father are not worth comparing to the reward of eternal fellowship with Him, then all the riches, comforts, and luxuries of a life lived in rebellion to the King of kings will not compare to the suffering of eternal separation from Him.

There are numerous times throughout Scripture where writers ask God why it is that the wicked seem to prosper while the righteous suffer. Often,

---

[30] 1 Corinthians 4:17-18

we may find ourselves likewise wondering why it is that those whom Jesus loves have to suffer for the mission of Christ and endure faithfully to the end, while those who live in abundance seem to have no issues even though they rebel against the God who provides for them. How do we keep from taking the posture of Job's wife in this scenario? How do we prevent ourselves from falling into the trap of believing that if this is how God rewards His faithful, we would be better off not worshiping Him at all?

By bringing to mind that God never abandons us to endure it alone, or lays the burden on our shoulders without providing the strength to persevere. All of Scripture is marked by even God's most beloved, suffering under extreme duress, and being sustained by His hand while He works His perfect will out in the midst of it all. Job in his loss, Elijah in his intense persecution, David as he was hunted by Saul, Jesus as He was crucified, the apostles as they were beaten, shipwrecked, poisoned, imprisoned and martyred for their faith. Job stands now as a glimmering testament to God's faithfulness and goodness. Elijah led a great spiritual reform in his nation which returned them to God so that the Lord may spare them and keep His promise of the coming savior in spite of their wickedness. By David's rule the nation of God's people was blessed for many years and by his bloodline all nations are blessed. By Jesus we have received our salvation, and by the faithful service of His apostles we know of His mighty work and can believe what we have heard to the glory of His name in all the Earth!

In all our trials, though we may feel as though we walk through a desert without end, God goes ahead of us as a pillar of fire by night and offers us shade as a pillar of cloud by day. He miraculously brings forth the manna in the morning, and brings water from the stone, and has given us the great cure for our most deadly ailment by lifting Christ high so that we can look to Him and be rescued![31]

Suffering itself is not a joyful experience or a desirable destination, but because God perfectly works all things for good, there are times where it is better that we suffer than be at ease. Obviously, this is a thought that is uncomfortable at the least and potentially offensive at the most. This is due in no small part to the fact that, as humans, we are naturally opposed to any suffering in our lives. An admission that suffering may be for our good in ways we could never fathom, and that God may at times permit suffering not in spite of His love for us but in *harmony* with His love is a tough pill to swallow. However, if we look at the story of Joseph in the Old Testament, we are faced with a clear indicator in what is perhaps the most famous passage of the story.

"As for you, you meant evil against me, but God meant it for good"
Genesis 50:20a (ESV)

God is not reactionary. He is not in the business of taking something that

---

[31] In order: Exodus 16, Exodus 17, and Numbers 21

has been thrust upon Him and trying desperately to make the most of it. He alone instigates, aligns, chooses, elects, and ordains by His own perfect will, and under no duress. There is not a force in all of creation which could place a set of circumstances into the hands of God and force Him to make do. So, God's intention *precedes* and *supersedes* the will of the wicked one.

This does not compromise God's perfectly good and holy nature. Although it can certainly feel that way when we are in the middle of difficult trials. Trying to apply this perception of suffering when we lose our job, or lose a child, or contract a horrible illness, is difficult to do. In those moments we must fight tooth and nail to keep God's Holy Word as the ultimate authority in our minds. It is a solid foundation, and if we trust that it is not only partially true but is entirely trustworthy, we can place our hope in its promises and not be put to shame. As we have already covered, defining God's nature by our circumstances is a surefire way to either lose our hope or be left with only a fool's hope to cling to. However, if we accept God's nature as the fundamental truth which is unaltered no matter our circumstances, then it radically redefines how we approach our suffering and equips us to rejoice in the midst of it.

Imagine a desert. A barren, arid, sweltering expanse of sand stretching out in every direction as far as the eye can see. In these types of places, what is it that animals do in order to survive? They migrate in search of life-sustaining water. These types of deserts may only have a handful of watering holes within a distance that the animals could realistically reach before the heat overcame them. The blistering sun overhead scorches and drives the creatures to the only place where springs of life exist. Animals are driven by the sheer brutality of their environment to that which will strengthen, sustain, and save them. They traverse and overcome mountains, valleys, and miles upon miles of unforgiving terrain just to reach the waterside and drink deeply.

If the animals had remained in relative comfort, undisturbed by the heat, they may not have been made aware of the pressing need of their own thirst. Then, by the time they became thirsty they would be too far from any water source to be able to quench their thirst before death overcame them. In the same manner that we see modeled in the natural realm with humans and animals alike, you do not need to feel your spiritual thirst in order to die from it. When people's bodies begin to shut down from illness or age, their brain ceases to recognize their need for food and water. In their own minds, they feel no hunger and no thirst, but they still need water and food all the same. This is why many people will actually die of starvation or thirst before their body succumbs to their ailment.

Jesus is our fountain of living water, and He dwells within our heart by His Holy Spirit. From its depths we can draw up peace, joy, and the strength to persevere. Unfortunately, for the time being it is housed within our weak and wayward flesh. It is contained in a heart which would much rather stretch out contentedly in the shaded protection from the sun's heat, than travel to the new place that Christ has called us and where He has sent His Spirit for us to follow.

The more scorching the fires in our life are, the more refreshing the Living Water tastes to our soul. The darker our surroundings, the more clearly we can see the radiant splendor of God.

God lovingly permits our suffering to bring us closer to Him, and by His perfect and beautiful will He uses it faithfully to burn away the dross from our justified and sanctifying souls. While our hearts have been transformed from stone to flesh, and the old self has been laid to rest beside Christ in His tomb, still we are being made new.

Comfort has seldom driven advancement, change, or improvement in any context. In fact, if you take a brief glimpse through history, or even as recently as in our modern culture, a glut of ease and comfort generally results in the stagnation and ultimate downfall of even the most powerful peoples. Broad and easy is the road which leads to our destruction.[32]

Our Heavenly Father has promised to provide for our needs, and He is both faithful and equipped to follow through on this promise. He is not a man that He should lie, and the storehouses of Heaven do not empty. However, we must recognize what our *need truly is*. We do not need a comfortable

---

[32] Matthew 7:13-14

and pleasant life free of any trials or tribulations. We do desperately and eternally need God. This is the ultimate matter of life or death in any person's life! Every time we share the Gospel it is a rescue mission, and when we submit our lives to Jesus for His Kingdom's cause it means that everything is now counted as lost for the sake of that mission. God loves us too much to allow us to go without recognizing that deep need for His salvation!

God does not permit our suffering out of vindictive or petty retribution against us. Even throughout the Old Testament, God's wrath is not poured out in spite, but in love and for justice. Your suffering is not evidence that God hates you or that God has abandoned you. This is especially true of those who have trusted in the saving work of Jesus Christ. What just God can rightly demand a penalty twice once the price has already been paid in full? To the embattled believer, know that your suffering is a tool for your good in the hands of the Lord, the one true God. While this world, our own flesh, and the agents of Hell may claw and tear at you, God is faithful to bring fruit out of the trials. If the blood of Abel cried out to God from the ground, how much more so will yours as the redeemed and beloved child of the King.

I cannot pretend to give a specific answer to every trial you will endure. I cannot tell you in particular detail why close friends betray us, why loved ones succumb to suicide, why spouses abandon marriages, or why mental and physical illnesses plague the body. Even Peter did not take it upon himself to specifically address the "various trials" which had afflicted his readers. He does not attempt to put words in God's mouth in the name of compassion for his brothers and sisters. It is far beyond my ability to speak on these matters in detail, but we can turn to the general revelation, lovingly found in Scriptures, which the Spirit applies to all our personal wounds. We know that suffering finds its origin in sin and its redemption in God.

This is the wonderful truth which Peter imparts to us in this passage. Accompanied by the reminder that God will one day not merely rescue us from our suffering, but He will remove suffering altogether. It will be so fully expunged that we will only even call it to memory in praises to God and remembrance of His faithfulness to us. Because of this mighty truth, Peter calls us to thought and resolve in 1 Peter 1:13. He says to his readers in this verse to, "prepare your minds for action". Or in other words, gird your mind for battle! Just because we have a steadfast and living hope does not mean that it will not be assailed. Peter issues a command to be sober-minded and to set our hope *fully* on the grace that is already within us and which will be fully realized when Christ returns at last.

Again, this is a call to *action*. Let our testing of God's promises be by our obedience to walk in the desert, instead of rebellion and remaining in the shade of our temporary comforts. Failure to place our hope on God means that we inevitably put it on shoulders that are too narrow to carry it and fall into despair and self-pity. A new creation in Christ is not made for despair! We are welcomed into a covenant relationship with the Prince of Peace and God of *all* hope. What defense can there be for a believer who wallows in their pain and sorrow, and never lifts their eyes to the hills for their Great Helper and Comforter? We are no longer spiritually dead, clinging to idols of money, power, and comfort in hopes that they will somehow spring to life and fight on our behalf against the waves of suffering which are crashing over us.

We are given a faith which is more valuable than all Earthly possessions. Faith which gives purpose to all of our suffering. Faith which makes it so that our pain bears fruit not only in our lives, but also in the lives of others. How incredible is the work of Christ, that even as we wait for His return our suffering is already being redeemed!

Do not be satisfied with suffering which merely ends. Because of Christ's work on the cross, all suffering eventually ends. Demand suffering that *matters* and hurt that is important and meaningful. Rejoice in pain that has value and isn't simply just a thing to avoid as much as possible until death takes us beyond its reach. If we suffer from today until the end of our lives, and all of our suffering is redeemed as even one stepping stone closer to Jehovah, that is of greater value than any measure of wealth or comfort God could possibly have blessed us with. This mentality requires a clear understanding and trust of the majesty of the imminent rescue in Jesus and the severity of the present threat of Hell apart from Him.

Every tear we shed in this life is worthwhile when it falls into the hands of a God who is faithful to work miracles with them. When our rugged hands are lifted in pleading, and He is enthroned on our praises in the midst of our grief, we lift Christ high so that others may trust in Him for their salvation as we have. Our enemies of flesh, world, and devil hurl suffering at us to shut our mouths and smother the light we carry. Our mighty King permits our suffering to raise our voices louder and to burn His light even brighter, We do not suffer in the same manner as the old flesh.

If I truly believe that Hell is the lake of fire, with eternal torment and separation from the presence of God, where worm and fire consume and there is crying and gnashing of teeth; if I truly believe that the threat of this fate is absolute and unflinching for the unbeliever, and that Christ has paved an escape route with His own blood then I cannot curse suffering that will help point the way to Christ for those who are damned to Hell. May I break every bone in my body, bear every illness, and suffer every indignity if even *one* person may receive the blood of Christ and be saved from eternal torment! Let me endure every torment if it causes the eyes of my heart to see more clearly the face and pierced hands of my mighty Savior. We ought to be willing to die a thousand deaths to spare even one soul from hellfire! If we actually trust the completed work of Christ as having secured our souls for eternal bliss, then the trade of our comfort for God's mission should be an exchange we joyfully accept.

Our most agonizing suffering serves the purpose of driving us closer to God, and we should covet no comfort in exchange. Because when we know God, we can walk through a kingdom of darkness filled with the lost and hurting. Like the beggar who has received bread, we can lead the suffering brother to where we have found *our* relief. We can cry out with confidence, "Come to my Lord! He is the Great Comforter. Come be comforted as I have been.".

Moreover, if our suffering drives us closer to God we can rejoice, because in exchange for our temporary pain we have received greater intimacy with the Almighty King of kings in whom we find all peace, joy, and satisfaction the likes of which we have never known. Is it not so like God, to give us such lopsided trades in our dealings with Him? We give Him our wretchedness and He gives us His love and salvation. We give Him our mourning and He turns it into dancing. We give Him our faithfulness in *temporary* pain and He gives us a relationship which stretches out into *eternity*.

As believers, we do not need to flee and avoid suffering at all costs. Because for us, this life is not all there is. In our faith we are at the very least able to endure all suffering by placing our hope in the eternal promise of Christ.

Going even further, we are able to rejoice in the midst of suffering because although we sow in tears, we will reap in joy.

Our pain does not produce bitter fruit. Pain itself is the bitter fruit of the sin which was planted in creation in Genesis 3. Much like the trees God has designed, which consume harmful carbon dioxide and produce life-giving oxygen for us to breathe, by God's miraculous power the believer can endure the pain brought on by the fall and produce a green flourishing life. This bitter sting of sin and suffering serves as the blistering sun which may drive us ever to the Living Waters of Jesus Christ.

By God's grace, we have never shed a wasted tear. You have never groaned in your agony alone before God. You can place all your hope on Him and He will bear you up to place one more foot in front of the other as He redeems every trial you walk through for revealing faith more precious than the finest gold.

Chapter 6

Where is Your Faith: Why hope when we are afraid?

Everyone has faith in or believes in *something*. Even if someone were to come up to you and say, "I do not believe in anything", they have put their faith in their own reasoning by default, believing that they are competent enough to rule out that anything outside of their own reason is deserving of their faith. This sets up a profound question which Jesus poses to His disciples on the Sea of Galilee in Luke 8:25.

"Where is your faith?".

It does not take a professional theologian to determine where Jesus' faith was. We can easily trace His faith to the Father simply by observing the resolve of His faith and hope. From this unshakable hope, Christ was able to command His followers, "Do not worry," and "Be anxious for nothing.". Were this teaching given in a vacuum, Jesus might rightly have been accused of being a fool at best or a cruel and unreasonable master at worst. If He were to issue such daunting commands without providing reasoning or help towards His weak children we might be forgiven for thinking, "Well that's easy for you to say. You're God!". Thankfully, this no worry mandate was preceded by a very important word. "Therefore". Because God is who He says He is, *therefore* do not be worried about what may come.

Admittedly, my original plan was to focus entirely on Matthew 6 and specifically the "do not be anxious" passage. This is a section of Scripture that has profoundly impacted my daily life since I first read it when I was about twelve years old. Naturally, my understanding of this passage has grown significantly, especially in the last few years as God worked to bring me from a position of optimism to a position of hope.

Growing up, my solution to anxiety or worry was simply to ignore it because God is bigger and greater. While this worked for many years, it became increasingly difficult once I had to experience actual life crises. When you have a wife, children, a job, and numerous other responsibilities, suddenly ignoring the dark clouds isn't quite so simple. Yet Christ's command still stands firm in the Word; do not be anxious for anything. To better explore the "therefore" that applies to the command to be anxious for nothing, we will be looking at a story from the Gospel of Luke.

"One day he got into a boat with his disciples, and he said to them, "Let us go across to the other side of the lake." So they set out, and as they sailed he fell asleep. And a windstorm came down on the lake, and they were filling with water and were in danger. And they went and woke him, saying, "Master, Master, we are perishing!" And he awoke and rebuked the wind and the raging waves, and they ceased, and there was a calm. He said to them, "Where is your faith?" And they were afraid, and they marveled, saying to one another, "Who then is this, that he commands even winds and water, and they obey him?""

Luke 8: 22-25 (ESV)

Stress and anxiety are not merely non-christian issues. We can look around and see many people in our lives suffering from some measure of anxiety or worry, both legitimate or contrived. Worry is a foul enemy which stains everything it touches in our life. It is an inky blackness which lurks in the periphery of every moment until it is dealt with. Even when we worship, pray, read the Word, and love God well, we will find every thought and deed marked with the fingerprints of this unwelcome intruder until it is dealt with.

Worry and anxiety are enemies that deserve to be cast out far from you and trodden under the heel of our Savior. Christianity is not a safe place for you to manage your triggers and quell your anxiety. It is a spiritual and at times physical warzone which demands that every time you wake up you must be prepared to suffer and die for the sake of the Eternal Kingdom and all the lost whom Christ is working to bring to Himself. Fortunately, I firmly believe that the mercy seat of God is a killing floor for all our infirmities where we can step into radical freedom. Otherwise, we will find our walk with God marred by the tendrils of the old flesh trying to wage war against God's sanctifying work in our hearts.

How? How does prayer liberate us from worry? How does Jesus' sacrifice free us from the grip of anxiety? How do we fight the creeping lies from the dark corners of our mind by shining the Light of God's Word into them? Why should we stop worrying? Because God is the cornerstone of Biblical Hope, we can wage war with divine confidence against every chemical, spiritual, natural, super-natural, genetic, or demonic fear.

At the beginning of Luke 8: 22-25 we immediately find a beautifully succinct summary of Christian life. Verse 22 should perk up your ears and put butterflies in your stomach. What the Spirit has done in v.22 is set the scene of a life spent in service to Christ. We find ourselves reading what essentially was a parable manifested into the real life experience of the disciples. One which can become a reliable retreat for the believer in times of trouble.

"He said to them, "Let us go to the other side of the lake""

Christians who have given their life in service to the Lord and accepted His gift of salvation are likewise submitted to the commands of Jesus. When He calls us up from the grave and into new life, we heed the call and the journey it includes. Contrary to what appears to be generally believed, we do not follow the Messiah into comfort and safety. In Jesus' command to His disciples, He does not say there is nothing worth worrying about, and so neither will I. God may very well call you into danger and lead you into difficulty. In fact, the more faithful the believer, the more likely these things will be present as they engage in actual war with the current world order.

When Christ was led by the Holy Spirit across the lake, the Spirit knew that there was a storm awaiting the disciples on their journey. In fact, we can infer that the storm did not happen in opposition to or in spite of God's will, as even the winds and the waves obey Him. So, knowing full well that a violent and dangerous storm awaited the party, the Spirit led Jesus and His disciples out onto the water. He *sent* Jesus into harm's way.

Jesus followed without protest or lingering.

"So they set out."

Here we can note the first encouragement for the believer who finds themselves beset by anxiety about politics, culture, finances, professional stresses, and kingdom service. Jesus said to His disciples "let *us* go" and now we see "*they* set out". Let it be remembered that God will not command us out onto the tumultuous waters where He will not go with us. Wherever the Spirit leads, He will go also!

Additionally, this serves as a sober teaching that the Christian is safer in the storm where the Spirit has led them, then they are on the beach where He has departed.

Remember that Jesus did not go into the dangerous and barren places so that we would never have to, but so that we *could go with confidence*, because we have a High Priest who can empathize with us in every way. He has made a way so that *when* we are led into the wilderness, we can depend upon Christ and His strength which is counted and not our own. We will not have to grope blindly in the dark because Christ has given us a lantern by which to see our next step. Jesus is the Prince of Peace, and His title is not primarily fulfilled by the removal of the circumstances which bring worry or anxiety. Instead, where Christ is there will be peace also, and since His Spirit abides in us our source of hope and peace is closer than our troubles.

Let's turn our attention now to the men who set sail with Jesus. Roughly one third of this group were fishermen by trade. Not only that, but they were fishermen who had grown up fishing in this very same sea. The Sea of Galilee where this story takes place is still known to this day for its sudden and unpredictable storms, brought on by the geographical layout of its surrounding environment. This unique obstacle can make it dangerous to cross, especially at night. Peter, Andrew, James, and John were not unaware of this fact. They were personally experienced with the hazards they might face if they chose to set out to sea with Jesus at this hour. It would have been far safer, more reasonable, and more sensible to shake Jesus' hand and clap His back saying, "You go ahead, Jesus. Make sure to let us know the next time you're in town.". After all, that's what everyone else did.

A "great crowd" had just heard the thunder of Heaven in this man's voice as He revealed the secrets of God and His Kingdom to them. He had worked miracles in their midst! He had healed the sick, cast out demons, and raised the dead to life before their very eyes. Person after person had been delivered from their agony by His hand. *Surely*, they could follow Him when He stretched His hand towards the water and said, "Let us go".

Their staying back teaches us something about our human nature. It is easy to follow Jesus on the riverbanks. We find little opposition in ourselves to believe in His authority, in His power, and in His love for us while the boat gently rocks in the shallows under the warm sun. It is comfortable to believe He is a "good man" and a "good teacher" when you are on the mountain top and held in His arms like a small child. We have no knowledge of our need for deep faith or hard teachings when nothing in our life challenges who we believe God is or what we believe His will looks like.

Those who are unwilling to press in and follow Jesus are those who remain on the shoreline, never stepping foot in the boat. This is important to remember, because it was not the people who remained behind that were led into a terrifying situation. It was not the people who turned away from following Jesus to find something better suited to their comfort levels who found themselves in the midst of a storm. Instead, it was those who followed Him faithfully and obediently who would come to fear for their very lives. It is not just the unrepentant or the weak Christian who takes on water in their lives and is bashed by the waves. The disciples in the boat with Jesus were just as terrified as the men in the boat a hundred yards away. We must be careful not to assume that terror in our lives is automatically evidence of distance from Jesus.

A storm in your life does not always mean you got into the wrong boat. It may very well mean that you got into the boat with Jesus when He told you to. There will be storms in your life that manifest specifically because you follow Jesus Christ.

While the world itself groans for its rebirth, the order of this world, a kingdom of darkness, wages war against the Kingdom of Heaven and the Bride of Christ. So, when we follow Jesus out onto the sea it is into the kingdom of darkness which would happily see us drowned beneath waves of sorrow, worry, and anxiety. We wade out into a culture which curses and flees God's rule, and persecutes the ambassadors of His Kingdom. In fact, Jesus' "do not worry" passage in Matthew is immediately preceded by Him *promising* that persecution would befall those who follow Him.

Quickly we see the faults of expecting a life without conflict because the Prince of Peace promises danger. Either there is a deep contradiction in the nature of Christ, or the peace He offers goes deeper than we may first suppose. A promise of peace is not the same as a promise of a peaceful life. We are in the middle of a war, where our enemy is desperate and knows his defeat is certain. Your entire life becomes a battlefield at conversion whether you acknowledge it or not. Yet it is in the same breath as this solemn forewarning that Christ issues His command, "Do not worry".

How many of us have heard that the Holy Spirit leads us to where there are storms, monsters, and where the kingdom of darkness reigns, so that we can wage bloody warfare against it and steal souls from the mouth of Hell? This is not necessarily an evangelism pitch you will readily find in many churches. Who have you told, or have you been told, that the only ones in physical peril in this story were the ones who were the obedient and faithful followers of Christ? The ones who were "safe" were in fact in dire spiritual straights.

While Jesus slept in the boat, a real and potent squall had begun to violently whip around Him and His companions. It raged with such ferocity that the seasoned fishermen who manned the boat became terrified for their lives and believed they were likely about to die. Despite their best efforts, the waves began to crash against the side of the boat, threatening to capsize it and sink them all.

As the night wore on, their predicament continued to escalate as the storm was a powerful force which they could not hope to oppose. Remember that Jesus said, "do not worry", He did not say we will never have anything worth worrying about. Luke does not say in this passage that the disciples "thought" their lives were in peril. Instead, he tells us that the boat began filling with water and that they *"were in danger"*.

These men had simply done as they were told by Jesus, and now they found themselves at the mercy of a force so powerful and so beyond them that they could scarcely hope to survive it, let alone overcome it.

Jesus continued to sleep. Why? Because the Spirit had called Him to the other side. The raging sea could have filled the boat to overflowing, and if need be, it would have defied the laws of nature and stayed afloat. Because Jesus had told them that they were going to the other side of the sea, they were going to make it no matter the amount of terrible force exerted against them. However, where Jesus had peace in the security of God's promises the disciples became afraid. Because in their eyes, the promises of God were not only distant, to their understanding they were entirely irreconcilable with their reality.

We too will falter in our courage when we allow our reality to dictate the trustworthiness of God to us. He has promised in Scripture that He will provide all that we need, but so many in this world go hungry, naked, and homeless. Perhaps even you have gone hungry, left to wonder where your daily bread is. Perhaps you have gone naked, and you have wondered how God can clothe the lilies of the field but apparently cannot be bothered to clothe His own child. Maybe you look around you and feel like you are bailing water 24/7 just to barely remain afloat. Wave after wave of family issues, abuse, manipulation, financial woes, addiction, betrayal, violence, loss, terror, and failure crash into your broadside and you are left feeling hopeless and helpless to turn the storm away. Forces beyond your control throw waves into your boat, and no sooner do you get a bucketful out then another wave pins you helplessly to the deck.

Know that your danger does not need to be smaller, more manageable, or even survivable for you to have hope and peace. Jesus shows us what it looks like to possess unshakable peace in the midst of turmoil.

The disciples were not unreasonable to be afraid of the storm. It is an easy matter to look at the wind and the waves and feel that worry and despair only make sense in such a scenario. However, what they say in their terror in the next verse betrays that their fear is grounded in the belief that the waves are more powerful, more real, and more present than the loving hand of God. They cry out, "Master, master we are perishing!". Mark's account of the event adds an accusatory tone to the cry, "Do you not care that we are perishing?".[33]

At first blush this may seem as though it is merely a genuine cry of distress to the One who could save them. They *are* in danger after all. Where is the problem then with voicing it to their Lord? I know that I have personally called out to God in much the same way many times in my life. I have cried out with tears of frustration, "Where are you Lord? My God, don't you care?".

---

[33] Mark 4:35-41

Let's look back to the passage and walk through it to see how Jesus responds to their disbelief and outcry for better understanding on how we can respond to our fearful ordeals. In v.24 we see that Jesus, "awoke and rebuked-" not their disbelief "-the wind and the raging waves". God's love for His children is such that He moved on their behalf while they are still caught up in their sin and doubt. Jesus did not *have* to act at all. He would have been within His rights as the Almighty King of the Universe to rebuke them for their disbelief, and walk onto the waves to the opposite shore while the sea claimed His faithless students.

How great is the kindness and patience of our Lord Jesus, that even when we curse His will in our worry and danger, He does not abandon us or leave us to strive in our own strength! Indeed, Jesus is a King with a heart of compassion. He sees first to our pain, our danger, our terror and lovingly corrects our hearts which have looked first to our problems and not to His glory.

Christ will not always stop the storm all at once as He does in this particular story. But the God who has authority over the wind and the waves is present with us in our greatest struggles. If they *must* obey His command to stop, then we can rest assured that they are not opposing His commands and rebelling against His authority when they rage. Our error, much like the disciples in this passage, arises when we are powerless to oppose the forces which threaten us, and we reach one of these two conclusions.

1. God is not keeping His promises even though He can.
2. Our problems are overpowering God because they can.

Both of these are terrifying prospects, and in the midst of our fear they begin to make a lot of sense and become almost inescapable. There are times when the Lord tarries in calming the storm, and we feel as though the weight of the world has been placed on our shoulders. Each step forward feels like it will be the last as we are slowly crushed beneath a weight we begin to doubt will ever be lifted. Sometimes God's rebuke to the storm is in a commanding voice which shakes the foundations of the Earth and causes the gales to fall silent in a moment. Sometimes the rebuke of the Lord is Him pushing His breath into your lungs again, pumping the lifeblood through your heart again, filling your mouth with a stubborn hallelujah again!

If the disciples had fought the sea all night long, believing that Jesus would bring them to where He had commanded them to follow, they would have made it to shore and survived the night. They would have awoken Jesus in the morning having believed in His word throughout the treacherous journey their obedience had led them on. Instead, they saw the wind and the waves and were overcome with fear. They cried to Jesus, not from desperate faith but out of fearful unbelief, "We are going to die! Don't you care?". This was not a cry for help, this was an accusation that their master had failed them.

Let us thank God that He does not respond to us in kind. Jesus' first response is one of grace and love. He wakes, and immediately rebukes the storm. Operating in perfect faith, power, and authority, He issues a rebuke which nature kneels to. Here we can note another lesson in the text. One that has convicted me greatly. Some storms in our life persist because we have not brought them to God.

We worry because like the disciples we struggle and strive in our own strength through the night and find ourselves woefully outmatched. We worry because we take up the fight and become convinced by the lie that God is not going to step in or else He would have by now. We believe that a good Christian or a strong person would be expected by God to handle things on their own. So, when we do everything we can and still find ourselves powerless against the raging sea, we become afraid that God has abandoned His disappointing child to their demise.

I am soundly convinced that the belief that God wants you to accomplish anything in your own strength or "by yourself" is a venomous lie which reeks of hellfire. This mentality that a mature believer handles all things in autonomy is us placing our natural understanding of maturation on top of our relationship with God. Scripture is opposed to this concept. We are told that the mature Christian is like a *child*.[34] This child must grow to eat the meat of Scripture and not only the milk, but the child of God does not outgrow the need for their Father. Let us not focus purely on the faith of a child as being unjaded and miss that it is also wholly trusting and dependent upon faithful parents to protect them and lead them into what is right.

After this miraculous display of His authority, Jesus turns to His wet and trembling disciples to pose the question which is at the core of this chapter.

"Where is your faith?"

This question cuts much deeper than simply asking why they did not believe in Jesus' words on the beach once the storm arose. If this was all there was to His inquiry He could have asked, "Why don't you have faith?". Was their faith in their ability and experience as fishermen? Was it in the circumstances when they set out, of calm waters and favorable winds? Was their faith placed in the reliability of the boat they had set out in? Pose this question to yourself, and allow honesty because it is a phenomenal indicator as to what the root of your fear actually is.

You can have more faith than anyone in the world, but even if your faith is as deep as the ocean and is placed in anything other than the Almighty King

---

[34] Matthew 18:3

of all creation, it can be shattered and overcome. For all your depth of faith there is nothing you can cling to in all the natural or supernatural world which cannot be overpowered, other than the Lord who sits enthroned above every other force and from whom *all* power finds its progenitor and master. This is why faith like a mustard seed that is placed in the Father can throw a mountain into the sea.

Jesus did not rebuke their desperation; He rebuked their misplaced faith. Their faith was not *in Him*, it was thrown *on Him* as a last ditch effort. How many of us likewise relegate Jesus in our lives to a "Break Glass in Case of Emergency" savior? When we place our faith in our strength, circumstances, or ability, we give God secondhand faith when all those things fail to measure up.

He's not *really* where our faith is; He is the object of our faith but not the source. So, once whatever our faith is actually in crumbles, we find ourselves disillusioned with God. A perfect example of this is when you ask someone who has left the faith why they did, and you receive some variation of, "God did not (   ).", and then you can fill in the blank. What this betrays is that their faith was not actually *in* God, it was in the blank.

We can turn this question around on ourselves if we want to get really uncomfortable. Ask yourself, why do you continue to believe in God. See if your faith is actually in something other than who He is. Such people may very well have deep affection for God, but that is not the same as having made Him the source of their faith.

When we are stripped of our false anchors of faith and cry out to God in desperation, He does not remain silent or distant from us! He does not punish His children for their crying out in danger, but He does offer a rebuke in pointing to why the wind and the waves were able to capsize our faith.

He illuminates how it came to be that we could be convinced to believe the threats of the enemy over the promises of our Savior.

Death itself may be at the door, but the King who holds the key to the grave and has ripped out its teeth is Immanuel, God with us. He is good in the spring showers and in the hurricanes. His will is done in the summer breeze, and He speaks peace and comfort from the whirlwind. Our God is not so small that His love can be driven out by our pain. So why be afraid, if anything that comes to us has done so by the Father's hands? After all He is a good Father. He is faithful to take every bitter moment I endure, and fashion it into a crown of glory which I will lay at the pierced feet of Jesus when all pain is at last removed for eternity.

Call to God in your time of need, and do not believe for a second that He does not draw near to you. Do not let your enemy convince you that the storm on the horizon means that your God has forsaken you. The Shepherd will never lead His flock beyond His reach. On the highest mountaintops and in the darkest valleys, God is there with you and for you.

Jesus always had the authority to calm the storm, but he slept because He was at peace with the Father's will. The foundation of His faith was not in the weather, in the boat, in His disciples' ability as sailors, or even in His own power or strength. It was placed in the God who called Him out into the storm, and as such it could not be shaken.

All of the disciples' fretting and fear could not keep a drop of water out of the boat. It did not turn away a single wave or offer a break from the gale. Likewise, our anxiety cannot alter a moment of the storms in our lives for the better. But the faith and trust which Jesus placed in God afforded Him peace and rest in the midst of the storm. All worrying accomplishes is fixing our eyes on the storm clouds, rather than the infinite I AM who is in the boat beside us.

The one who is closer than a brother and our genuine help in our deepest need abides in us! If He does not calm the storm it is not because He is too distant, too small, or spiteful, it is because He is too loving to stop it before all the good that will be wrought by His hand has been done. In faith I can cry out to my God and trust that if the storm stops it is His good will towards me, and if it persists it His good will towards me. I will trust that the Omniscient God knows better how to give me what I need than I know how to ask for what I need.

We only know how to ask for the needs which we can identify, but God knows the full depth of our need and is faithful to provide for them even through that which seeks to do us harm. If the storm remains, then we need what the Lord is doing in the midst of it because He is faithfully fulfilling His promises to us *through* the storm. Faith in God produces an unshakable foundation to our hope that stands firm against the threats of our enemy. In Biblical Hope we find the ability to sleep in the storm.

Chapter 7

Waiting Not Weary: Why hope when we are waiting?

Waiting.

There have been many seasons in my life where I have had to wait. As someone with high ambition and a desire for action, this is an obstacle that I tend to struggle greatly with anytime it comes around. Waiting usually brings with it a feeling of tension. Sometimes it can be an uncomfortable tension, such as one which accompanies an awkward silence. Other times we experience a thrilling tension. One that excites us and is full of anticipation as we look forward to something wonderful. A perfect example of the latter is to think of a child counting down the days to Christmas morning. Even now as an adult, I love and look forward to Christmas. With the joy of the season, the time spent in the company of friends and family, and with the long-held traditions which are enjoyed by all, it is easily one of my favorite holidays.

One of the Christmas traditions that my family had when I was growing up was that my mother would disguise our presents to prevent us from guessing what my parents had bought for us. She began this tradition out of necessity because my brothers and I had become adept at deducing what our gifts were. She employed several strategies to conceal the nature of the gifts, from putting marbles in them for added noise, to using disproportionately large boxes to wrap them, to placing heavy rocks inside to throw off the weight. Sometimes we would try for days to discover what gifts were held in these doctored packages!

Occasionally we would manage to guess one or two, but most of the time we would be left wondering all the way up to Christmas morning. As I reminisced on these happy memories, a question came to mind. What is it that made not knowing what was in the box a matter of thrilling tension instead of anxious tension? If I do not know what is in the box, why am I excited?

During this tension, the time of not knowing and having to wait for everything to finally be revealed, my brothers and I had to trust that the love of our parents would mean that whether we knew what specifically was hidden in the box, it would be thoughtful and loving, and would come about in its proper time. No amount of waiting or confusion was going to make me question my parents' love for me, because I was reminded of it on a daily basis.

Knowing who I waited on impacted the way that I waited. It made it so that I could wait with eagerness rather than anxiety.

Let us look to the book of Isaiah for further clarity on this.

"Why do you say, O Jacob, and speak, O Israel, "My way is hidden from the LORD, and my right is disregarded by my God"? Have you not known?

Have you not heard? The LORD is the everlasting God, the Creator of the ends of the earth. He does not faint or grow weary; his understanding is unsearchable. He gives power to the faint, and to him who has no might he increases strength. Even youths shall faint and be weary, and young men shall fall exhausted; but they who wait for the LORD shall renew their strength; they shall mount up with wings like eagles; they shall run and not be weary; they shall walk and not faint."
Isaiah 40:27-31 (ESV)

This relationship between what we wait for and who we wait on and its influence over our waiting is why we see God say things like, "Have you not seen", and "Have you not heard". He reminds His people of who He is, and what He has done. Because who we wait on is more important than what we wait for. We do not wait on a small God. We do not wait on a cruel God.

We do not wait on a God from whom we have to pry blessings from with a crowbar. God is a King, but He is not a politician. He makes His promises with both the intention and the desire to fulfill them. That is, in a nutshell, why we should have hope when we are waiting.

Have you not seen? Have you not heard?

The Lord, of course, knows the answer to these questions. All of Israel had heard of the might of Jehovah. For generations, the history of their people had been passed down; about the God who led them out of Egypt, who established all of creation by His Word and power, who had made a covenant with their father Abraham, and who had saved Noah from the flood which cleansed the Earth.

They knew of what God had done in days gone by, but they had failed in growing to know Him as a child knows their Father! More important to them than what God had done was what He was presently leaving undone. Their displeasure with their waiting had risen to such a peak that they began to believe that their frustration gave them just cause to question the nature of their God.

Christians, do we not know, or have we not heard of the promises secured by Christ Jesus for His people? Of course we have! For two thousand years we have declared His promises, and for two thousand years God has kept His Word and His people. The promises we wait for now are secured by the promises which have *already* been fulfilled.

Believers are equipped to carry on in our waiting because we wait on the Everlasting God. He has faithfully displayed His nature throughout all of human history, without failing. His unsearchable understanding has never been stumped or confounded by enemy or circumstance. We wait on a God who has promised not only that He *can* move, but that He *will* move. We wait on a God who has declared that He will redeem all things. If any portion of Scripture is true and worthy of our trust, then so must this be.

Just as we cannot pick and choose from the commands of Scripture according to our comfort level in obeying them, neither can we pick and choose from the promises of Scripture according to our comfort level in believing them.

Now what does this mean for the person who grows weary with waiting? How are we supposed to wait and remain steadfast in hope? How can we keep clinging to God when we are beset on all sides by enemies and find our every weakness exploited as we desperately strive to keep moving forward in righteous anticipation? Well, what does God do for the faint, according to this passage?

He gives *power* to the faint!

When the burden that you carry is crushing you underneath its weight. When you find yourself pinned by the might of every lengthy struggle which seems to consume each day and stretch on with no foreseeable end in sight. Are you afraid that you have been knocked down with so much force that you may never manage to rise from it again and just desperately wish that the fight would at long last be over? Jehovah gives power to *you*!

He blesses you with the power that you need to be able to stand and lift that burden back onto your shoulders; to keep pressing forwards to Home. With a burst of divine vitality, He will set you on your feet again, dusting off your despair, and even though you may feel as though at any moment you will faint and be all at once shattered beyond saving, in a moment He will give you the power necessary to stand up under the burden again.

God gives power first, because there is little use in giving strength to someone who has been so burdened that they cannot even lift themselves let alone press on in their journey. He does also give strength to us who have no might so that we can carry our burdens, but before you can carry one you need the power to lift it. Beautifully, the power that is given by God is indeed His own. The very same power which sent forth a command into a vast nothingness and from His power there erupted everything that now exists! Reality itself cannot resist this power. Sin and death cannot overcome this chain breaking power which pierced the veil to the Holy of Holies, and which raised Jesus Christ out of the grave. If you are faint in your waiting, this power is given to you!

Cry out to the Lord! Depend on Him! It is a damnable lie that God helps those who help themselves. God helps those who call upon His name and walk in the faith that He is sure to answer them. Humble yourself and lean on Him fully. Do not come to Him as though He serves to supplement your strength, but with the knowledge that He *is* your strength. He will not grow weary of your weakness or resent your dependency upon Him. In fact, it is by His design that we come to Him to lay hold of the daily renewed mercies of God. He gives power to the faint.

Are you without might? Do you feel discouraged and weak in the face of the waiting and long arduous road you see stretched out in front of you? Maybe you have already received the divinely powerful push from God, and you have shouldered the pack once again. Your cross is on your back, but your feet seem rooted to the spot, unable to take a single step further in the hope of coming blessings or relief. To those who have no might, God gives *increasing* strength. Strength that is always sufficient for the task at hand,.

God does not merely stop at giving you the power to push back, but He also grants you the strength to press on. Just as He gives of His own power, He likewise gives us strength from the everlasting pool of His own might.

Do not simply brush this aside as a trite platitude of the Church. Hear it and receive it! Out of God's everlasting, unlimited, and unsearchable might He gives us strength. Meaning we can call out to Him every year, every month, day after day, and moment after moment throughout our entire lives and He will never tire of giving His strength, and indeed His stores will not even be diminished at all by His generosity. You can throw the bucket down the well a million times and if the well is bottomless, the bucket will never return empty. The depths of our God's strength are inexhaustible!

Moreover, this promise is not meant simply for the old and weary sojourner to lay hold of. Many of us have likely felt at times that our problems are too small to bring before God Almighty. Or maybe we have considered our state of affairs and thought that since so many have waited longer than us, and for greater relief, we must certainly hold out much longer before crying out to our Heavenly Father. Yet in this passage we are told that "Even youths shall faint and be weary".

To the feet of God is the only distance your own strength has to carry you before you cry out to Him.

Plead before the throne when you wake up in the morning. Pray for His provision of strength as you drive to work. Before you have lifted a finger for the day or exerted yourself in any capacity, praise God for His sustaining mercies which are already prepared afresh before the sun has even risen. There is no milestone that your own strength must carry you to before you are permitted to depend on Jehovah Jireh.[35]

While it is true that at the end of yourself you will find the Lord waiting there for you, it is not as though we reach Calvary on our own. Wherever you fall, you fall at the foot of the cross. No matter how far you have attempted to run from God, or how far you have tried to strive towards Him under your own strength, when your knees finally hit the ground, there you will find the feet of Jesus Christ, Son of God and Friend of Sinners.

Everyone has the need for His divine aid the same way they need air to live.

---

[35] Genesis 22:14

The grace and strength of God is the oxygen in the lungs of our new flesh, and apart from God's generous mercies our faith would die outright without our managing to stumble two steps in the right direction under our own might. Isaiah's declaration that even youths will grow faint and be weary is a comfort to the weak and a rebuke to the haughty. Those who seem powerful to the weary are just as desperately in need of grace as their "weaker" brother. There is no shame in calling out to our Mighty Father, knowing that we cannot carry on alone.

To the professing Christian who sees no need to depend on the divine outpouring of strength, you must ask yourself if you are indeed walking on the Lord's path. Because God seldom, if ever, leads you down a path where your own might is enough. What good does that do for you? What benefit is that to anyone else? If you look at those who are calling upon the name of the Lord and do not feel your own heart crying out in concert with them, beware that you may very well be traveling under your own strength.

The danger of this course being that when we walk under our own might, we work diligently to chart our own course, where our might will be sufficient. To those who carry on, walking down the wide and easy path, turn and climb onto the narrow way! You are not supposed to be enough. Why would you settle for what you can attain by your own strength and in your own timing instead of waiting and relying upon the Lord? Why would you not surrender to His timing and depend on His strength? No doubt your answer would be some version of the one which I have often given myself.

Trusting God is terrifying.

Even once we have trusted in God for our salvation, taking the step into genuine, bare-all, surrendering, naked, vulnerable, unhindered trust with every aspect of ourselves is a terrifying concept. In fact, if we are honest, many of us are not even that open with our own spouses, who we can see and touch. How much more frightening is the concept of trusting the invisible God with such abandon?

God is of course perfect in love and righteousness, completely trustworthy now and forever. However, this rarely makes our transition any easier or more comfortable from guarded to vulnerable, from doubtful to trusting, or from autonomous to dependent. But be assured that avoiding that transition handicaps us in a war against darkness in which we need every advantage.

Around mid-2019, my wife and I learned that she was pregnant again and that we were to be expecting our second child. Whereas the positive pregnancy test for our first daughter had been met with excitement, laughing, jumping, and perhaps some colorful language, this time we immediately collapsed into each other's arms. We wept and praised God for

His goodness and this beautiful gift we had received. Children are a gift from the Lord according to Scripture, and a positive pregnancy test is a good reason to celebrate for any parent. Family and friends rejoiced with us as many people have throughout history, and we wept because *at long last* we were receiving a gift that we had waited four years to receive.

This pregnancy was not a surprise, in the sense that we had been keeping our eye on the horizon for its coming quite a while. We had waited several years to hold another positive pregnancy test in our hands. There had been four years of trying and waiting. Four years of sleepless nights spent pleading with God when month after month, nature took its course and signaled an empty womb. I cannot count the number of times I came before the throne of God in painful prayer during those years. After comforting my heartbroken wife, I would come to my knees and beg God to fulfill the promise He had given us, that we would indeed have more children.

We *knew* God was faithful, and that is fairly easy to believe in year one. It got a bit harder in year two. Once year three rolled, around we were having to work to maintain a glad heart whenever we were reminded of God's perfect timing. Well before year four, we were sick and tired of waiting.

We desperately wanted God to give us the power to overcome whatever stood in our path and was preventing us from conceiving. Everything was in working order, God had given us a promise, we had waited (mostly) patiently, we had called out to Him and *only Him* with faith that He alone opens and closes the womb, so what could *possibly* be preventing us from laying hold of God's gift other than an enemy?

It is all too easy when we face delays or opposition in pursuit of God's promises to assume that we are certainly opposed by our enemy. Seldom do we acknowledge that God may be delaying the prize in order to perfectly fulfill His promise.

When your friend keeps you back it is for your own good and not for your harm. We cannot assume that every delay is warfare *against* us. In fact, if God is indeed King of kings and Sovereign Lord, even the delays that are against us will be redeemed for us.

Many times, I prayed to God for the strength for us to overcome, but in His perfect love and eternal wisdom He instead gave us strength to endure. What's more, we were able to receive His strength and peace in greater measure once we at last trusted God with open hands. When we could pray for help and trust that whatever He saw fit to give in response was sufficient because our loving Savior would not jilt the children He died for.

As children of God, we must always be conscious of the posture of our hearts during the waiting. In the same way that the strength of God is not reserved for the ultra-holy and pious Christian, it is also not set aside for the petulant child who screams and yells and throws a fit in an effort to pry a promise from the hands of their Heavenly Father.

It is a *faithless* child who presses God to fulfill His own promises in the manner that *they* see fit. This is an image of a child who refuses to depend upon their Father. We must not forget that there is a difference between depending on God and mooching off God. A child who is dependent upon their parent makes no pretense of self-sufficiency. They possess a clear and present need which they cannot satisfy in their own strength or understanding, and therefore they submit to the will of the parent because they are the one who has the strength and understanding necessary to navigate the issue.

Meanwhile, a child who mooches off their parent desires all of the trappings of self-sufficiency, but wants it bankrolled by their parent. How often do we plot out our lives as though we are self-sufficient, with a vague trust that God will foot the bill for our ambition? Then, when everything fails to go according to our plan, we become restless and bitter towards God for having chosen to fulfill His promises in His perfect timing in accordance with His perfect will.

How often do we respond this way to our loving Father? Likely more than any of us care to admit. We must be aware of the posture of our heart, and learn to operate with the knowledge that even when we cannot understand God's actions or reasoning we can always trust His nature and His character.

Otherwise, once we press past our initial pleading with God in our waiting season, we will find that we become angry with Him. In those moments, our anger has actually shone a light on sin in our hearts. Am I saying that it is sin to at times grow discouraged in our waiting? Of course not. However, when our waiting causes us to become bitter or distrustful towards God, it ought to be a red flag to us that perhaps we have been trusting incorrectly. Or even worse still, maybe we were never actually trusting God in our waiting at all. It is possible that we have actually been waiting on what we want *from* God.

If what we want from God is the anchor and foundation of our perseverance instead of God Himself, then we have been worshiping the promise rather than the promise giver. This is a tiring and futile method of enduring to the end, and since God is a jealous God you can believe that He will not spare your feelings in tearing down your idols.[36]

Hoping on what we believe God *ought* to do will paint a picture for us of a faithless, forgetful, failure of a God as the days stack up. We will grow weary of faithfully waiting when God continues to move as He wills and not as we will. When we decide in our hearts that the fullest expression of God's goodness and faithfulness is manifested in Him doing *what* we want Him to do *when* we want Him to do it, we rob Him of His divinity. Meaning when God as He is does not match up with God as we want Him to be, it is not hard to stumble into believing that He may not be God at all.

---

[36] Exodus 20:5

Too often I find my prayers for strength, for might, and for victory revolve around my interpretations of God's beautiful promises. I want the blessing without the waiting. It should really be no surprise to us that when we make demands of God without submitting to His will or timing, we find ourselves exhausted by the struggle. We absolutely ought to depend on God, and we certainly should make our supplications known to Him. However, relying on God and submitting to God are not necessarily the same thing. Waiting on the Lord involves dependence, but it also demands submission. To put it frankly, waiting on the Lord requires waiting.

Those who *wait* upon the Lord *will receive.*

Those who trust, rely upon, submit to, and follow God will receive His strength and His might. If God has set you in a place of waiting, how can you expect His blessing if you decide to press on ahead by yourself? He does not give His strength to the stubborn child who rebels against His will and calls it sacrifice. It is the child who trusts that the Father is who He says He is, and will do what He says He will do, who receives strength to do what their King has required of them.

They will not turn or run when the enemy comes with his boasts, and his threats, and his lies. When the devil tells us that we have been abandoned to fend for ourselves, we remind him that we have not been left as orphans.[37]

---

[37] John 14:18

When the world lays out alternate paths for us to walk down, all of which seem to point directly to where we most desire to go, the child who trusts that only God can faithfully lead us to what He has set aside for us and through the lands He has called us into receives the strength for their journey!

This is the Word of the Lord, given without abstraction or vague wording, that those who wait on the Lord *will* have their strength renewed. When God gives a promise, rest assured that it is already done.

He exists eternally and outside of time, while we are presently bound to our linear time with beginning and end. Therefore, when God gives a promise, it is instantaneously fulfilled and we just have to reach the day when our lives intersect with God's perfect timing. That is how sure we can be in our waiting, and why our hope should never flag when time seems to drag on without fulfillment.

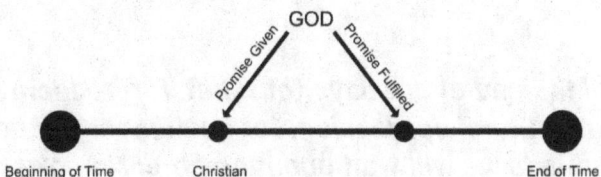

My wife and I were able to endure through that difficult season of four years spent waiting because whenever we came to the feet of God in our tiredness, in our frustration, and even in our anger, by God's grace we were resolved to wait upon the Lord. To not only trust Him with the victory but also with the battle. Because He is trustworthy. Because He is faithful. Because He is God, and we are not.

Those who wait on the Lord *will* renew their strength. Note that God has used absolute language in this passage. He does not say "may" or "can". The only qualifier in this passage is who it is meant for, namely those who wait on the Lord. There is no room left for questioning otherwise. God has bound Himself to His own Word by using absolute language. They *will* renew their strength.

How do we have Biblical hope while we wait? By waiting on the Lord. By asking Him for the power to rise when we have been struck down and relying on Him for strength to put one foot in front of the other as long as needed. By remembering that God makes a promise and fulfills it at the same time, the only delay is in our reaching it, and He is faithful to redeem that journey.

If we wait until the end of our days for relief, for freedom from supernatural and natural oppression, for healing for our bodies, hearts, and minds we will wait upon the Lord! No power in Heaven, on Earth, or from the pits of Hell can outlast the power and strength of the Almighty God or overthrow His promises to us.

This can be difficult ground to stand on, and we may often feel as though we are not strong enough to endure in faith. I have wonderful news for you!

Come to God in humility, patience, and submission and you will not have to be strong enough. The faint receive power and those without might receive strength. Those on the brink of defeat God fills with divine vigor and sets on their feet. If this describes you, then there is only one more quality standing between you and seizing this promise.

Be one who waits upon the Lord.

Chapter 8

Faithful in Faltering: Why hope when we fail?

Back when I was in middle school, and fresh on the social media scene, Facebook had a feature where you could set up a quiz to test how well your online friends actually knew you. There were several questions that you could choose from, and you had the option to fill out multiple choice answers. The only question that I actually remember from that quiz was "What is Caleb afraid of?". I remember mulling this question over in my highly advanced and mature 14-year-old brain. There were honestly not that many "standard" fears which affected me much. I was the designated bug-killer in our house, I loved roller coasters, and I loved climbing tall trees. By all accounts, I was a regular suburban daredevil. So, to begin with I wanted to give my friends a few answers that were clearly wrong.

1. Bears

There were no bears to concern myself with where I grew up. This was not even remotely a realistic threat, and in my mind it made no sense to be afraid of it.

2. Spiders

Again, I was the designated bug-killer in my family. A fear of spiders was not a luxury that I could afford in my line of work.

Once I had taken care of the two easy answers, I thought it was probably a good choice to add in a more feasible answer as a red herring to make the quiz more challenging. I tried to formulate the perfect answer which would *sound* correct to somebody who knows me. In an uncommon moment of teenage lucidity, I concocted the third choice.

   3.   Letting down the people who depend on me.

...

   4.   Nothing!

Self-awareness rapidly dissipated, and I entered the *obviously* correct answer that there was in fact nothing in this world which made me afraid. Everyone who took the quiz selected "D", and affirmed my macho-ness, except for my father. Because in all honesty he knew me much better than I cared to admit.

He selected "C". Ever since childhood, failure has been my greatest fear in life. This has manifested to varying degrees, and I have managed to master it in many areas of my life. But it is easy for *anyone* to feel the sting of failure and allow it to evolve into guilt and shame. This is especially true when we sin against God.

Whenever we allow the voices of guilt and shame to become the voices that we listen to in the midst of our failure, instead of pushing towards God, we will find ourselves withdrawing from Him.

There is a story near the very end of the Gospel of John which exemplifies this and which I have rarely heard taught in Church. It is the story of Peter's reconciliation to Jesus.

There was a precise question which prompted me to find this story in the first place.

"Why did *Peter* have to betray Jesus?"

Peter was arguably the most zealous and fervent of all of Christ's disciples. He loved Christ aggressively, and many times said in not quite so many words that *no one* loved Jesus the way that he loved Jesus, and that he would never leave Him.[38] Be that as it may, immortalized in each of the four Gospels is the story of how Peter ultimately denied Jesus to strangers three times in order to protect himself from shame and harm.[39] What could possibly be the redemptive reason for Peter of all people to fail God in this way? Not only failing Him, but his failing is made all the more severe by the oaths of loyalty he had given. Then I realized that if Peter had not failed so severely, then Scripture would only have one example for how to respond if we fail our Lord Jesus Christ. That would be the example set by Judas.[40]

The story of Peter's reconciliation to Jesus after his denial is a somewhat

---

[38] Matthew 26:35
[39] Matthew 26:69-75
[40] Matthew 26:14-16

lengthy passage, but I think it would do us well to read it in its entirety as it is rich with details that we will be diving into to find our own source of Biblical hope when we fail.

"After this Jesus revealed Himself again to the disciples by the Sea of Tiberias, and He revealed Himself in this way. Simon Peter, Thomas (called the Twin), Nathanael of Cana in Galilee, the sons of Zebedee, and two other of His disciples were together. Simon Peter said to them, "I am going fishing." They said to him, "We will go with you." They went out and got into the boat, but that night they caught nothing.

Just as day was breaking, Jesus stood on the shore; yet the disciples did not know that it was Jesus. Jesus said to them, "Children, do you have any fish?" They answered Him, "No." He said to them, "Cast the net on the right side of the boat, and you will find some." So they cast it, and now they were not able to haul it in, because of the quantity of fish. The disciple whom Jesus loved therefore said to Peter, "It is the Lord!" When Simon Peter heard that it was the Lord, he put on his outer garment, for he was stripped for work, and threw himself into the sea. The other disciples came into the boat, dragging the net full of fish, for they were not far from the land, but a hundred yards off.

When they got out on land, they saw a charcoal fire in place, with fish laid out on it, and bread. Jesus said to them, "Bring some of the fish that you have just caught." So Simon Peter went aboard and hauled the net ashore, full of large fish, 153 of them. And although there were so many, the net was not torn. Jesus said to them, "Come and have breakfast." Now none of the disciples dared ask Him, "Who are you?" They knew it was the Lord. Jesus came and took the bread and gave it to them, and so with the fish. This was now the third time that Jesus was revealed to the disciples after He was raised from the dead.

When they had finished breakfast, Jesus said to Simon Peter, "Simon, son of John, do you love me more than these?" He said to Him, "Yes, Lord; you know that I love you." He said to him, "Feed my lambs." He said to him a second time, "Simon, son of John, do you love me?" He said to Him, "Yes, Lord; you know that I love you." He said to him, "Tend my sheep." He said to him the third time, "Simon, son of John, do you love me?" Peter was grieved because He said to him the third time, "Do you love me?" and he said to Him, "Lord, you know everything; you know that I love you." Jesus said to him, "Feed my sheep. Truly, truly, I say to you, when you were young, you used to dress yourself and walk wherever you wanted, but when you are old, you will stretch out your hands, and another will dress you and carry you where you do not want to go." (This He said to show by what kind of death he was to glorify God.) And after saying this He said to him, "Follow me.""

John 21:1-19 (ESV)

Right away, in the first verse and again in verse 14, there is something to note about this passage. At the time this story takes place, Jesus has already revealed Himself and visited His gathered disciples twice, making this story the third time He has visited them since His resurrection.[41] However, this is the first account of one of His visits where we find *Peter* present and involved in the narrative. In Christ's previous two visitations Peter never came forward.

Placing ourselves in Peter's place, it is not hard to imagine that he was hindered and kept back by the weight of his own shame. He likely convinced himself that Jesus had come to see the other disciples, the faithful ones, and that he had just happened to be in the room when Jesus came to speak with the disciples who had not betrayed Him. We can find clues that lend weight to the theory that Peter had not engaged with Christ during these moments, even though we have it written that he was present in the room.

Firstly, whenever Peter did *anything* in the Gospels, it was mentioned in the narrative, and in the accounts of the prior two revelations of the resurrected Christ there is no word of any action on his part. Secondly, Jesus chooses this time to address Peter's denial, meaning that they had not yet spoken of it together or dealt with it.

---

[41] John 20:19-29

Because of this we can gather from context that this time on the boat was when Peter at long last decided to engage the resurrected Messiah. He had decided that the shame of his failure would no longer be a barrier keeping him from encountering the Lord whom he had loved so dearly.

Until now, Peter has concealed himself from his Lord the same way that Adam and Eve did in the garden[42]. He has withdrawn from the King he betrayed, and his guilt has constructed a wall which has kept him from going to Jesus. It is easy when you fail to believe that God may *love* you, but He doesn't love *you*. Thoughts like this had poisoned my relationship with God for many years without my knowledge.

I believed the lie that God hated me.

You see, Satan is a master deceiver who specializes in taking a sliver of truth, twisting it and perverting it in order to have us believe his lies. For example, he uses the truth of how good, and awesome, and worthy God is, and how deserving He is of my love and devotion, to press me to begin going so far as hating myself whenever I failed or sinned against the Lord.

Then, in the same manner as Peter, I would withdraw from Him, convinced that He is merely obliged to love me because He is bound by His nature. He must love me because He is love, but He tolerates a relationship with me at

---

[42] Genesis 3:8

best, and even that may change if I were to fail too severely or too frequently. I would not be surprised if most of us hold a similar view of our relationship with God.

Even believers who know that Scripture paints a beautiful picture of the love of God which is neither acquired nor secured by works can still be burdened with a belief that the affection of God is very much dependent on how good we are.

Failure, as I am using it here, is not simply when we "drop the ball". When I say failure, I am also referring to marriage ruining, job losing, relationship wrecking, life altering, irreversible failure in our lives. There is hope found here and elsewhere in Scripture which can radically transform the outcome as truth intersects our failing and God meets us in our weakness. Why is this story so impactful? Because it is one of the key hinge points in Peter's life.

This is the moment when he will either be accepted by Christ, or he will be rejected. This is when he will need to decide to be open and vulnerable with his Lord, or withdraw in despair. What we are left with is an encounter which is the defining interaction where Peter's story and the story of Judas are made separate.

Judas was so overcome with despair and self-loathing in his failure that the only relief or justice that he could conceive of was for him to die, and if no one else was going to exact justice on him then he resolved to do it himself.

So severe was his failing, that he knew he deserved the death penalty for having betrayed an innocent man to die. When those who were supposed to safeguard the law refused to take action against him, he slew himself out of desperate shame. Judas had no hope in his failure. He was a murderer and a traitor of the Messiah! He had betrayed the King for the price of a slave. Almost in a mirror image, Peter denied his King, and even went so far as to call down curses on his own head if he were found to be a liar when he said, "I do not know Him."

No wonder Peter had not approached Jesus until now! He was rooted in his failure, with his mouth shut up by his own shame. Jesus' foretelling of Peter's denial surely rang in his mind, turning and sickening his stomach at the memory of having fulfilled the prophecy, having denied Christ as fiercely as he had claimed to love Him. Imagine how it must have felt. Waiting moment by moment for when Jesus would at last turn His eyes on Peter and send him away from the house and fellowship of disciples. The same way that Cain was sent away from his family[43]. Waiting to be cut off from the Kingdom in the same way Saul had the kingdom of Israel torn from him.[44]

Or perhaps he expected that Jesus would shut him out, and remain silent as God had remained silent in Israel after she had whored after her idols and

---

[43] Genesis 4:16
[44] 1 Samuel 15:28

murdered His prophets.[45] Waiting to be sent away as he had seen false disciple after false disciple sent away as they were found to be without genuine faith.[46] Peter waited for Jesus to look him in the eye and send him out into the streets alone. Preparing to wander for the rest of his life with only the memory of fellowship with the Godman who had so radically transformed his life.

Once, Jesus had come and did not reject Peter or send him away.

Twice, He had come and still not rebuked Peter for his sin. He had not cursed Peter or cast him out of His presence.

Without waiting for another visitation, Peter opted to return to where Jesus had originally found him. He went away from where Jesus had appeared to His disciples and set himself back to work fishing, the only thing he really knew how to do. Only he was again met by continued frustration. Despite spending all night fishing, he worked in vain and caught nothing. There Peter was, failing again. This time he was failing at the one thing he was confident he could actually do well!

Then, in the midst of his failure, when he had gone out in his own way, a man calls to him from the shore. Miraculously, this man fills their empty nets with fish, and Peter's mind does not make the connection or recognize

---

[45] Malachi 4:5-6
[46] John 6:60

that this is the very same Jesus whom he feared would deny him. After all, Jesus had said, "Those who deny me, I will deny before my Father.".[47] But once John told him that this mysterious man on the shore was in fact the Lord, he did not hesitate, and he threw himself into the sea. His shame could not keep him back any longer.

Three times Peter had denied Christ, and now three times Jesus had come. This third visit, Jesus did not come to the group of His disciples, but He came for Peter! In the previous visitations Peter could have easily supposed that his own presence when Jesus appeared was a mere coincidence of timing. But this time *he was the one* who had decided to go fishing. None of the disciples would have been out on the sea that morning if not for his choice. Now he could be sure that Jesus had sought *him* out.

Peter was not about to let another opportunity pass him by. The Lord was on the shore. So, Peter was going to the shore! Jesus welcomed His denier to come into a place where He had prepared food for them all. There wasn't just enough breakfast for Jesus, or for Jesus and the other disciples. Christ had prepared a place for Peter as well. Whereas Peter had drawn back, Jesus had drawn near.

Jesus then told Peter to go and bring the fish that they had caught, even though John tells us that He already had everything ready when the

---

[47] Matthew 10:33 (abridged)

fishermen came to shore. There was no need for Peter to bring the fish as any sort of provision or addition to what Christ had already prepared. Nonetheless when Jesus told them, "Bring some of the fish." Peter hauled the filled nets ashore, which six other men had not been able to pull into the boat without assistance.

I took some time to look up how much weight Peter may have been pulling in this net. The "large fish" they caught would likely have been the Biny Fish. which ranges from 13-15 pounds each. This means that the net could have easily weighed as much as two thousand pounds!

Peter, in his obedience to the command of Jesus, was pulling ashore an embodiment of his grief, his guilt, and his shame. John 21 also tells us that in spite of this great weight, the nets did not break. Metaphorically we know then that not one bit of Peter's sin would not be caught up in the grace of Christ. It was a burden that no one could have borne, but at Christ's command he brought it forward. As I mentioned, these fish were not needed for provision. So it was that Jesus gave Peter the chance to bring the great weight of his failure and set it at the feet of his Savior in a place of welcoming and provision. Peter did not allow the opportunity to pass him by.

After all of this, we finally reach the exchange which Peter had surely been dreading. Jesus asks him, by his original name, "Simon, son of John, do you love me?" Peter had reached the point where he was going to be brought face to face with his failure by the One whom he had failed. There would be no more avoiding it.

This is the manner of how we come to Christ in repentance. He welcomes us, but if you have truly come to the feet of the God of Scripture, then He will not permit your sin to go without being confronted.

No sooner would a doctor leave a tumor on the heart of his patient then God would leave sin in the heart of His child. He makes a place for us and welcomes us as we are, but He will never leave us as we are.

"Do you love me?"

How many times have you asked yourself this same thing? "Do I love God?" Personally, I have agonized over this question.

Peter had failed not just a king, but *the King of kings*. He had buckled under the weight of his fear and his weakness, and he had forsaken his great friend. We are in Peter's place anytime we sin and rebel against our God. There he was, at the ultimate tipping point of his life.

Jesus asks Peter, "Do you (Agape) love me?", and Peter replies to Him, "Yes Lord, you know that I (Phileo) love you."

While I do not want to place an undue level of emphasis on the different words used in this conversation, it certainly warrants our attention. Jesus asks Simon Peter if he loves Him unconditionally. Peter's response can be read almost as though he is pleading with the Lord saying, "Please, you know that you are my dear friend!".

His answer repeats when Jesus asks him once again, "Do you (Agape) love me?" Then John tells us that Jesus asks Peter this question a third time, and Peter is grieved, as the parallel to his own denial of Christ three times certainly is not lost on him.

However, it goes even deeper than that, because in His last question Jesus also used Phileo love. "Are you my friend?" Three times Peter had denied his love for his friend, three times Jesus had sought him out, and now for a third time Jesus asks Peter if he loves Him. Peter's two-part response to this last question is powerful.

"Lord, you know everything".

Lord, you know my sin, you know my weakness, you know my cowardice, and you know my betrayal. There is nothing that is hidden from you O God! All that I am is laid bare before your sight. There is nothing in the darkest corners of my heart that you have not seen and that you do not fully know. I cannot hope to conceal my sin from you.

"You know that I (Phileo) love you.".

Repentance should sound like this. It should sound like coming to the Lord and crying out, "Lord, you know my every sin, and you know that I love you!"

Instead of sitting in our boat, trying to draw up our sins from the depths under our own strength, we ought to have as much to do with the retribution of our sins as Peter had with the fish in his nets.

It was Jesus who brought them to the surface, it was Jesus who made sure that they were gathered up securely to be dealt with, and it was Jesus who requested that Peter bring them over to Him. Peter obeyed, and at Jesus' command he dragged the mighty weight to the feet of God. He then sat with the Lord in loving fellowship, invited there by his King and friend.

What a beautiful picture is painted here of our salvation! To labor all the night long without success, and to have Jesus appear to us at the breaking dawn of the new day. At His word, the work is finished.

Do we respond the same way Peter does when Jesus calls to us from the shore? Do we throw ourselves headlong into the sea without a moment's hesitation and swim with all our might until we are kneeling before Him?

Does His amazing grace move us with this same power? That once we recognize His presence, we abandon all hope of laboring under our own strength and flee to Him; where He has prepared a place for us even in our waywardness.

We can do this, and we can do it with confidence. Because even in this story when Peter has failed, betrayed, and abandoned the Lord Jesus Christ, he is not sent away. Jesus does not condemn Peter to death as an earthly king would do to any deserter. No, in fact He responds by doing two beautifully loving things for Peter.

Firstly, Christ addresses Peter's sin. Even though there are other disciples gathered nearby, it is more than likely that only Peter would catch the full meaning of Christ's questions at this time. Three times Jesus asked Peter if he loved Him, and it unmistakably echoed Peter's cowardly denial of Him when He had been arrested. This was not done to shame Peter, but to strip away any remaining veil there may have been between the two of them.

Our feeble attempts to shroud God's vision and obscure His ability to address our sins as we try to draw near only serve to hinder our ability to draw close to Him. Jesus knew this, and so He lovingly laid bare the guilt and sin which sat like a burning wound in Peter's chest. Peter was now at his most vulnerable before the Lord.

Graciously, God does not strip us of our filthy rags in order to laugh at us in our nakedness, but He does so to make us clean and clothe us in righteousness. Placing His own robe on our shoulders, and His ring on our finger.[48] Welcoming us back to where we belong.

Secondly, Jesus foretells Peter's death at the hands of murderous men. You would not be out of line for thinking that this sounds much more like a punishment for Peter's previous denial of Him than it does a loving word. As though this were some kind consequence or retribution for his cowardice.

This is how I thought of this passage for much of my life as a Christian. I imagined that if Peter had just kept his act together, then there was an option for a future free of this martyrdom that now awaited him, but because he had failed so spectacularly Jesus had given him a future as a martyr as penance. While Jesus' prophecy foretells Peter's death, where he would be bound, imprisoned, and taken away to be executed, this death was not because Peter had betrayed Jesus. It was to bring glory to God.

God was going to work through Peter in such mighty ways that the kingdom of darkness would have to assassinate him just to be rid of him. His death would be a testament to the might of the glorious Heavenly Father, who could use a fisherman, zealous and weak, to rain terror down

---

[48] Luke 15:11-32

on the heads of Satan and his allies.

If Peter's death had nothing to do with punishment, do you know when the debt of his sinful betrayal was actually dealt with?

There on the beach in Galilee, when he jumped out into the sea and swam to Jesus. He came out of the midst of his failures and flocked to the resurrected Christ, who had already made a place for him before his feet ever touched the shore. Jesus had told him to bring forth what signified the impossible weight of his own sins. He did not then task Peter with carrying it away and disposing of it himself. Nor did He command that Peter carry it around with him wherever he went. Jesus asked Peter to bring this incredible burden to *Him*.

After Jesus had hosted His disciples, His attention turned to Peter alone. Jesus singled Peter out so clearly, that it is included in the Gospel account of John, who was the only Gospel writer present at the time. Jesus had come here to bring His child back to Himself. Then, after addressing Peter's sin and affirming the call on his life, Jesus speaks two beautiful words.

"Follow me."

How wonderful a command this is! Jesus has set the table for the weak, the cowardly, the traitors, and the failures. He calls us all to come and to eat with Him. His own disciples now occupied the seats of the tax collectors, the prostitutes, and the thieves whom He had broken bread with so frequently during His ministry. Not only do we receive divine hospitality at the feet of Christ, but we also receive an invitation to relationship.

Remember, this was the same command that Jesus had given Peter when they first met on the shores of the Sea of Galilee.[49] Jesus' love for Peter was unchanged from the start. Before Peter had done anything to "earn it", Jesus loved him. Now after Peter had done everything to lose it, Jesus loved him just the same and once again told him, "Follow me".

Something we must grasp is that the love and the affection of God are not separate or independent from one another. I once believed that God loved me by necessity of His nature, but due to my own nature I would never be able to attain His affection. I believed that while God may love me, He certainly didn't like me.

The truth is that if I cannot make God quit being the lover of my soul, then I can certainly not make Him stop calling me His friend.

My previous model of repentance had consisted of heaping shame and guilt on myself until I felt that I could justly approach the throne of God, and that He would find my repentance was genuine and He could feel appeased enough to forgive me. Like Peter, I labored all through the night, only I did

---

[49] Matthew 4:18-22

not recognize that I was drawing up nothing despite all my efforts. This model, which I thought produced genuine faith, had actually only served to place a wall of despair between me and my loving Savior.

I couldn't hear Jesus' call of greeting from the shore, because I was too busy screaming abuses at myself and agonizing over my shortcomings. Jesus' model of relationship with us creates a distinction between guilt that we heap on ourselves, and conviction which is of the Holy Spirit. Whereas one follows a pattern of shame, hate, and despair, His method is one of conviction, love, and hope.

Jesus loves us the same, as He loved Peter the same, because His love has never been dictated by our successes or our failures. He is God! He makes His decisions by His own counsel alone, and so just as we cannot cause Him to love us, we cannot convince Him to do otherwise. God loves you because of who He is. Since He will never change, neither will His reason for loving you.

You have a greater chance of snuffing out the furthest star with your fingertips than you do of extinguishing the love of your Heavenly Father with your failures.

This love does not merely cover minor mistakes, as love covers a multitude of sins.[50] Even our most catastrophic failures in life are forgiven by Jesus Christ. Because not only is God able to save the worst of the wicked, but He

---

[50] 1 Peter 4:8

desires to do so. This can be a tremendous stumbling block for believers who feel that their failings may put them outside the affections of the Father. We know that God is *able* to save, we even know that He *will* save because of His faithfulness to the promises made to those who call upon the name of Jesus, but we are hard-pressed to ever believe that God *wants* to save us. To believe that He desires us.

God *wants* the liar, the cheat, the coward, the murderer, and the failure to be rescued to Himself. He sent Jesus for the express purpose that the worst of humanity could be saved and brought into His family. It was His directive, His mission to seek out the wretched and the very least of us to invite us in for the mighty feast His Father has prepared.[51] Will you continue to hide your shame from Him who desires to wash it clean?

Jesus stood on the shoreline, and Peter leapt into the sea to swim to meet Him, because His beloved Savior had sought him out. If you are hopeless, believing that God will only ever begrudgingly accept you, then I would like you to walk with me through the miracle that you are even reading this chapter at all. God has ordained and directed your birth as well as my own.

He has preserved my life, at least long enough to have written this book, and likewise He has preserved your life long enough to read it. This has included His holding back of both natural and supernatural forces which

---

[51] Luke 14:15-24

would have liked to kill one or both of us, or at the very least have derailed this particular overlapping of our lives. Paper had to be invented, as did ink, as did the written language or languages, as did the printing press. Not only for this book to be written, but for the Word of God which has inspired everything within this book to have been produced on such a scale that I could have accessed it at all.

If you are reading this in print, then the publisher had to have worked with a manufacturer to compile all the needed components in such a way as to produce the book you are holding. A delivery truck, powered by prehistoric vegetation running through an internal combustion engine had to transport it. Businesses had to develop in just such a way as to produce, sell, and deliver this book into your hands. Do not even get me started down the rabbit hole of the technological advancements and intricacies involved if you happen to be reading a digital copy.

God stands on the shores in this book, and He has sought you out. Jesus died with eyes wide open. There was no dark corner of ourselves which He was not entirely aware of before He even stepped down from His throne and into Mary's womb. Christ has made a place for you, and in His great love He bids you to bring all of your sins to His feet. In His great affection for you He says again, "Follow me".

Chapter 9

Kingdom Come: Why hope at all?

So far in this book I have worked to lay out our Biblical cause for hope in various circumstances we might find ourselves in throughout life. Now I would like to pull our view back some and look at Biblical hope from a grander perspective. Why should we have hope in the first place? What security do we have which provides us with a legitimate reason to have hope which can carry us through the eventualities listed in the chapters above?

Our answer, in short, the foundation of our hope is the Promise Keeper and His promises.

Are there promises or is there a specific promise which can serve as the foundation of our hope? Thankfully there is such a promise, and it is reiterated in part or in whole multiple times throughout the Scriptures. Within our main text for this chapter we can find helpful encouragement that will display the beauty of the promise which has been made to us as well as the unfaltering trustworthiness of the Promise Giver.

"Then I saw a new heaven and a new earth, for the first heaven and the first earth had passed away, and the sea was no more.And I saw the holy city, new Jerusalem, coming down out of heaven from God, prepared as a bride adorned for her husband.And I heard a loud voice from the throne saying,

"Behold, the dwelling place of God is with man. He will dwell with them, and they will be his people, and God himself will be with them as their God. He will wipe away every tear from their eyes, and death shall be no more, neither shall there be mourning, nor crying, nor pain anymore, for the former things have passed away."

And he who was seated on the throne said, "Behold, I am making all things new." Also he said, "Write this down, for these words are trustworthy and true." And he said to me, "It is done! I am the Alpha and the Omega, the beginning and the end. To the thirsty I will give from the spring of the water of life without payment. The one who conquers will have this heritage, and I will be his God and he will be my son. But as for the cowardly, the faithless, the detestable, as for murderers, the sexually immoral, sorcerers, idolaters, and all liars, their portion will be in the lake that burns with fire and sulfur, which is the second death." "

Revelation 21:1-8 (ESV)

Our initial glimpse of the coming promise, in this passage, is a grand one to behold. Immediately we are greeted by the descending of New Jerusalem, a gift from God to His people, shimmering in splendor as He steps down to dwell among them forever more.

It is lowered by His hand, ready and waiting to be filled by His children's homecoming. This is not a project that will have been thrown together on the last day in a slapdash manner, but rather it has been carefully prepared by the Father for the dwelling place of the Groom and His Bride. The coming of this city is inevitable. Since before the beginning of time it has been prepared and adorned for the Holy Day when the wedding feast of the Lamb arrives, and the Lord descends to live among His people at long last![52]

No longer will we be constrained to a crooked and flawed imitation of life as it is in Heaven. The Kingdom of Heaven will wholly swallow up the kingdom of darkness and overcome it until God's reign is fully manifested on the Earth. The separation created by the fall of man will be lifted and we will be able to dwell in the unfiltered presence of the Lord, and live![53] Sin will be stripped away from the fabric of creation forever, and that divine fellowship with God will be restored to what it was always meant to be.

Jehovah is the master storyteller, and I do not think it is by coincidence that here at the very end of Scripture we find the enduring promise of God which was always fulfilled from before the beginning. His promise that the Almighty will make His home among His people. That our skin will be warmed by His light as it is now by the sunshine on a cloudless summer day. That our days and nights will be illuminated by the closeness of His glory, and we will never again have need of sun, or moon, or stars.

---

[52] Revelation 13:8
[53] Exodus 33:20

Never again will chaos or division turn brother against brother. Never again will the blood of innocents be spilled by the machine of war. We will no longer squabble amongst ourselves over the nuances of God's divine nature. His people will be reunited with their King, and at long last cast off the shackles of sin, emerging from the grave as Lazarus did and breathing the fresh air of fully realized eternal freedom. Our God will mend the created order with the blood of Christ and all will be made right.

There is not another religious figure who can claim to have desired, planned for, or promised to redeem and physically join a rebellious and wicked creation, and dwell in their midst for all eternity. What we see in Revelation is that God has planned it from before time's foundation to return as a Father does to His children. Jesus waits eagerly to return as a Bridegroom to His Bride. This ought to stir up a thrill of joy and spark a roaring fire of hope in our hearts!

The Lord is prepared and ready for His entry! He has never set aside His crown. His throne is ready to be placed on the soil of the Earth He created. Even now, He holds His holy city in waiting, and He will not permit a moment to pass beyond His perfect design before He flies to the relief of His long-suffering people.

People will claim that they wrestle with trusting and submitting to God because they feel that He has made Himself distant from us, if He exists at all. Even many who profess faith in Him will stop short of believing that He is truly involved intimately with the daily affairs of their lives or the world at large.

Those who have a high view of His character and His glory, and a right view of the fallen state our lives and world exist in, may even seem to approve of God's distance because why would He ever *want* to become involved? Surely, God would never truly *desire* such foul people or such a wretched world with so much sin and suffering. Certainly, He paved the road to salvation out of the goodness of His nature, and not from the affection of His heart.

At this point, it can be easy for a person to lose nearly all hope in a joyful Christian life, and trudge through their trials as mandatory service to a far-off King until at last they are removed from it all. This posture can even manufacture a false sense of enlightenment or spiritual maturity to a believer who has resigned themselves to diligent and joyless service.

Acknowledging God's authority and obeying Him are the most rudimentary seeds of wisdom which the Holy Spirit places in our hearts at birth. What a depressing thought to suppose that it is the extent of His desire for us!

God fashioned life that is wholly dependent upon His constant attention or else it will all fall apart in an instant. If He withdrew the breath He gave, *all* creation would wither. God's desire has always been to live among His people. It was the original created order before sin fractured it. It is the taste the Israelites received through the Ark of the Covenant and the prophets. It is the taste which we receive now in the indwelling of the Holy Spirit. It is the aim and purpose to which He has fashioned all of history to lead towards.

Everything from Eden to Golgotha leads to Jesus' sacrifice of self to secure the restoration and perfection of that original design. Every New Testament promise points back to that great sacrifice and forward to His return.

It would be as foolish to believe that God does not desire an intimate relationship with His creation as it would be to believe that there is no God at all. Because in rejecting God as He has revealed Himself to be, we have replaced Him with a god we more easily accept and believe in. I would go so far as to suggest that it is idolatry for a Christian to believe that they are not a precious son or daughter of God.

Idolatry that is focused on whatever version of God they find truer than how YHWH Himself has been revealed in His Living Word. There is little wonder that such people find so little hope in their trials. Because if God can love us without being kind or caring towards us, then we have little reason to believe that He will help us, rescue us, or redeem our pain for good.

Praise God that this is not the truth! Rejoice that God is on His way! I can suffer every indignity, every pain, and the deepest grief when I know that the faithful God has promised me eternity in His presence. This is why a believer's eschatology (our beliefs about the afterlife and end of time) is so vital to our daily walk with Christ. Because our view of then informs our view of now. With an eye on the scope of eternity, everything which currently looms over us is dwarfed by comparison.

Eternity in the New Heavens and New Earth is so much more than "merely" life without sin, death, sorrow, or pain. It is so much more than "merely" having the freedom to enjoy the created universe as it was originally designed to be.

We will not simply be spending eternity enjoying all these physical and spiritual comforts, because every physical blessing received will one day, be it in a year or a trillion years' time, run dry of joy and wonder to provide by itself. Just as a skydiver can eventually become immune to the thrill of hurtling towards the Earth, and in the same way that eating your favorite meal every day would eventually cause you to grow tired of it. These things, while wonderful, only have so much joy to give.

Beyond all those blessings, God has given us Himself. The eternal, uncreated, Almighty God who is in every way everlasting. We will at last be able to encounter Him without a single impediment and we will have all of eternity to delve into His being and still we will never reach the end of His glory or the joys and wonders that His nature has to offer. It is the first promise of eternity and of our new world, and it is by far the greatest.

Every other blessing flows out of this initial promise that God will be among us and that He will be our God. Jesus lived, died, and rose again to secure this promise for us. To make the lowly and wretched holy in the sight of the Most High so that we could live in His presence.

As citizens of the Kingdom of Heaven and as children of the King of kings we will receive the fullness of our promised inheritance. These promises are not earned by outward living. Acting and mimicking the culture of the Kingdom will not grant this inheritance. Lip service and outward deeds do not change whose name you bear or what kingdom you belong to.

Who is your Father?

Jesus rebukes hypocrites for being outwardly clean, but in reality, being sons of Satan.[54] Is your blood the blood of the Lord or the deceiver? Are you kin to the King or the betrayer? You will go where your father goes. Those who have submitted wholly to Christ as Lord and received His sufficient sacrifice for their pardon, have also been made co-heirs with His inheritance.

---

[54] John 8:39-47

Scripture tells us that we are His Bride, and the Bride and the Groom are made one flesh receiving and sharing in all things with one another. Therefore, if you are married to Christ in that Divine Union, what has been given to Him has likewise been given to you. If you have been rescued from Hell's fury, then you have been brought to the beautiful gates of the New Jerusalem where we only need wait for it to open.

"He will wipe away every tear"

Countless years of grief and pain will at last have reached their end. Sorrow will be lifted away forever by the hand of God, and we will know only the sweetest joy forevermore. Joy so profound that were our natural heart tasked with holding it then it would burst. All at once we will rejoice in the agonies endured because we will see the fulfillment of God's redeeming work in them. Our lamenting will be turned to praise, and our mourning into dancing. When we go home, all the evil of our suffering will be lifted and only the good will remain. Like dross being burned away we will be left with the beautiful gold.

God will kneel down Himself, as a Father with His child, and will lift your sorrows off you forever. As He has longed to do, He will do at last, and we will know that every painful moment was worthwhile.

"Death will be no more"

Death's sting has been removed, and its teeth have all been pulled, but soon it will be done away with entirely once and for all. There will no longer be illness which invades our bodies and the bodies of our loved ones. No longer will we have the need to fear loss, or dread the grief that our own departure will one day force upon those we hold dear. Death will be cast out, no longer serving any purpose except for when we recall it to sing of God's victory over the grave.

"Neither shall there be mourning, nor crying, nor pain anymore"

Not only will God remove the sting of our past sorrows, but in His presence we will never taste them afresh. We will never again receive fresh wounds to our hearts or bodies. Pain is going to fade into memory. Even these reminders of God's deity and our humanity will pass away because we will dwell in His presence. In the light of His glory there is neither space nor need for such reminders.

"For the former things have passed away"

The way things are done "now" will become the way things were done "then". Every twisted symptom of the fallen world will be stripped away, like a field which is presently overgrown by thorns and weeds. The Lord will purge it all and in its stead He brings what is beautiful and life-giving. Not only will the old things be defeated, they will be removed and replaced.

The mission and foregone victory of the Kingdom of Heaven is the glorification of God and the restoration of all things. Meanwhile the kingdom of this world, the kingdom of darkness, is the kingdom of former things. We must be mindful of where our citizenship is truly found. If we cling to the former things, and bitterly refuse to let them go, then we will surely pass away with them in the end.

There is no place for a rebel heart in the Kingdom of Heaven, and there is no allowance for contraband from the kingdom of darkness.

We will not be able to smuggle even our smallest idols into the New World with us. If we tie ourselves to them, we will find ourselves on the outside looking in when the gates are closed. For a time, God has allowed the rebel and the idolater to coexist with His people for their benefit, but on the Day of the Lord they will be removed.

Realize that God is not coming to "reclaim" His throne. There is a general behavior as though God is presently a displaced ruler who will be returning to reclaim His Kingdom and set Himself on the throne again. Would it be any wonder that such beliefs would cause us to struggle to hope, to willfully put our sin to death, and to serve Him wholeheartedly?

A displaced leader does not inspire us to hope or to fear Him as we ought to. Remember then that God has never left His throne! Now and always, He has been and will remain the King of kings and the Lord of lords on the Throne above every other throne. At this very moment He is seated there. Never for a moment has He been supplanted in power or authority. He is not coming to take His *power* back: He is coming to take His wayward *people* back.

Because of this, instead of being hopeless people, we should have all the more reason to be filled with hope. Not only *will* He redeem all things, but even now He is "making all things new".[55] God is taking what has been broken and ruined; the universe, the world, us, and He is making them new, showing us yet again an example of His great love and affection for us.

It is one thing for a creation to be completely replaced. This type of replacement is seen by example of the New Jerusalem being lowered from the Heavens down to Earth. It is another thing entirely for something that is weathered and broken to be made new. God's design and desire is not to dispose of this world for a new one. He does not want to toss His people aside and fashion replacements. Rather He is even now working all things together to restore this world and His children to their complete design.

An example of how God's redemptive work is currently taking place while we are still waiting for it to come to fruition is to picture baking a cake. When baking a cake, you would need to gather eggs, flour, milk, sugar, and

---

[55] Isaiah 43:19

any other ingredients you may need. Once the first egg is cracked, or the first scoop of flour is dumped into the mixing bowl you are officially in the process of making all of the ingredients cake. Nobody may be able to tell that when they watch you beat the eggs, or in stirring the batter, or in preheating the oven, but when the timer finally sounds off at the appointed time you will be able to see that the entire process consists of making all ingredients cake. Likewise, God is invisibly authoring all of creation throughout history as He makes all things new.

Every second that passes God is about His mighty work. Time will land upon the Day of the Lord like a fleet of ships on a homeland shore, and we will set foot in the land where we belong for the first time. Like Noah and his family who emerged from the ark not to the sight of a broken or replaced world, but to one which had been cleansed and made new.[56]

This may very well all sound too good to be true. It may even strike you as immaterial or perhaps metaphorical; something that has no bearing on the here and now because we are at a loss to ever possibly substantiate it.

In fairness, were we to approach these promises in a vacuum or even merely in desperation we can find it difficult to cling to them or find any real comfort in them. How can we possibly have confidence in these promises? How can we graduate from the ignorant school of optimism and

---

[56] Genesis 8:6-12

be galvanized against our trials by the wash of Divine Hope? We must look at the context of the promises, and most of all we must look at who the promise giver is.

Because hope is only as strong as whatever it is placed in, and a promise is only as trustworthy as the one who is responsible for keeping it.

Firstly, note that it is not the Apostle John making these promises on behalf of God. It may seem like a minor detail, and one which may have even slipped your attention, but it is critical. Picture the televangelists and prosperity preachers who swear up and down that God has promised to provide you with health, wealth, and happiness. They make promises on behalf of God which cannot be substantiated and more often than not are proven to be untrue by time and experience.

John does not act autonomously. Rather he is recording, at God's request, what He Himself is saying to His children. God intentionally makes a simple yet impactful command and claim when He tells John, "Write this down, for these words are trustworthy and true." He has in effect tied the honor of His own name to the promises that will follow, and lent His trustworthiness to them.

As the Creator and all-powerful God, who is Truth, who cannot lie, and whose Word and power uphold all of creation and keep it together, if God says something is true all of reality must conform to what He has said.

Because God is Truth, everything He says must be true or else He would cease to be God. If Jehovah can be dishonest, deceived, or ignorant, then He would cease to be worthy of our adoration as He would cease to be the infallible and all-powerful God. He would no longer be the supreme being and would at best be a powerful being who could be overcome. A King who can be overthrown cannot be a steadfast assurance. His Lordship cannot serve as the collateral for our hope if He is anything other than the omniscient, omnipresent, omnipotent, supreme God.

In the verse immediately following God's command to John, we receive a bold statement in two parts which seals the security of our hope in this life.

"It is done! I am the Alpha and the Omega."

Here we learn that not only is the promise of restoration, relationship, and relief true, but it has already been accomplished! This is a unique attribute found in the promises of God, which was addressed in our chapter on waiting, and is only made possible by His existence as an eternal and uncreated being; the Alpha and Omega. He exists outside the constraints which time places on you or me. Once again I will share the rough diagram of how we might understand how God can claim in truth that this redemptive work has been accomplished while we wait for His return.

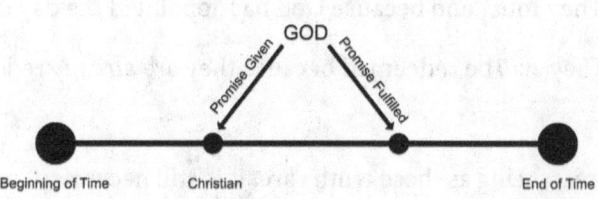

The illustration assumes or simplifies time as linear. There is a clear beginning, this can be assumed and is also supported by Scripture, and likewise there will be (or is) an end. Because all of time, from its beginning (Alpha) to its end (Omega) exists within God's power, and He Himself exists outside of the reach of its influence.

As a writer would be intimately involved in the machinations of a narrative without being bound by it in the same manner as his characters, what God has promised is already done. It is already set as completed work in a fixed point of time; we just have to reach it. So it is that God can claim that the renewing of all things is already done. What greater source of confidence could we ask for? Is there any greater anchor for our hope than to know that not only will God be faithful to fulfill His promises, they are actually already fulfilled?

This is the reason we can hope. God will not and cannot forget, fail, or forsake us because He has already kept His promise of the great restoring work! Because of this, we can persevere through any and every trial. Each trial or suffering season is assured by God, swearing by His own name, to come to an end. They must end because God has appointed the day of their ultimate defeat. They *will* be redeemed because they are *already* redeemed.

As beautiful and reassuring as these truths are, it is still necessary to add one further point of context. It is not enough to merely know the promise and the Promise Keeper. We must also factor in who is the beneficiary of these promises. Who are the promises made to?

"To the thirsty I will give"

A dead body does not thirst. Corpses cannot come pleading to the Master of the Streams of Living Water in search of relief. Moreover, the rotting cadaver would not be able to do anything with the waters it may receive. Those renewed into spiritual life will receive freely from the Lord. Everything about the Kingdom coming on the horizon is concerning the spiritually alive. We must take stock of our hearts, and as Paul says we need to work out our salvation with fear and trembling.[57]

Do you desperately thirst for God's streams of living water, or do you merely fear the flames of hell? If we consider our afterlife, eternal pleasures are clearly far more appealing than torments, but if you do not ache for the presence of the Lord, to draw deeply of Life Himself, then be cautious as it is possible your spirit has not yet been raised to life.

Living spirits will desire the presence of the Lord. Not without fault and not

---

[57] Philippians 2:12

without failure as we are still burdened with our sinful flesh, filled with lusts that work day and night to pull our affections away from the God who deserves them. A heart with no aching, a soul with no instinctual supernatural yearning for God Himself may very well do all it can to flee Hell and even go so far as to work tirelessly to live a "good life" and only be trying in vain to run away from the lake of fire, which is not the same as running towards the River of Life.

Living spirits thirst as they grow parched from the warfare they must wage in their own members, against the world, and against Satan and his legions. Make no mistake that all of these forces work daily to snatch your inheritance away from you or to keep you in bondage to the kingdom that is passing away. The moment you are raised to life you are called out of the grave and onto a battlefield for the rest of your natural life, against forces of the kingdom of darkness with the sole intent of seeing you thrown into the pit alongside them.

Truly it is not God who desires to see us cast into Hell, but the very pleasures and idols we covet which work to pull us into that eternal prison. They come to us and barter with their fleeting pleasures as Jacob did with Esau[58]. Where Esau traded his inheritance for a bowl of soup and we mock him, yet we are so keen to turn away from the eternal heritage of Christ and His divine inheritance and pursue carnal things of little to no value.

---

[58] Genesis 25:31

Many are content to spend all their days spitting in the eye of their Heavenly Father and trading their inheritance for a bowl of lusts, greed, deceit, and self-rule.

We have an enemy who knows how weak we are to the yearnings of the flesh. So, like Jacob, he comes to us and freely offers what our flesh hungers for, and all we must do to lay hold of the carnal is to relinquish the holy.

By the power of God's Holy Spirit, by His daily renewed mercies, and by His fully sufficient grace we conquer and overcome. Continuously we press forward and march to claim what has been given to us as God's chosen people. In the same way as the Israelites took possession of the land the Lord had given to them.[59] As conquerors we also subdue and overcome the forces which rise up against us and our purpose.

For one to be considered a conqueror there must be an opposing force or forces which are conquered. What are these spiritual Canaanites which oppose the regenerate Christian?

Our Carnal Self:
By the cleansing and reviving work of the Spirit, we bear His fruit in our lives and our carnal self is conquered and overcome day by day. Our greed, dishonesty, idolatry, pride, lust, and anger are conquered as we crusade to the Kingdom of Heaven.

---

[59] Joshua 1:15-17

Satan and His Kingdom:

Untold hordes of spiritual foes rally against us and wage their war against our divine mission. They seek not only to turn us back and beat us down, but to keep us from multiplying on the Earth. Make no mistake, these creatures are older and more powerful than you or me. Yet in Christ we will be more than conquerors, for the creature is no match for the Creator!

The Present World Order:

Our current world order is a supernatural system of government which has been twisted by the fall and pressures us daily towards the mouth of Hell and away from the gates of Heaven. Have you ever wondered why sin is pleasurable and plentiful while righteousness is painful and scarce? It is because the created order has been corrupted by sin, and in its fractured state it rages in opposition to its King and His people.

By Christ's work and the quickening of His Spirit we are reborn into this hostile territory. As a once wicked soldier, upon our conversion what once was our fortress becomes a camp behind enemy lines and we must now make our way home through a wicked and treacherous land. From its onset, the life of a believer is a warpath homeward. This may sound like an impossible path fraught with insurmountable obstacles, and believe me, for the unregenerate man or woman it is.

Just as a corpse cannot scale a mountain, and just as a dead man floats downstream without even the pretense of protest, so the unregenerate will find themselves hopelessly overwhelmed by their foes as they seek to flee the threat of Hell.

Where then, do we find our hope? Our hope is found, for the regenerate believer, in the truth that Jehovah is God and that we are His adopted and beloved children, eternally secured by the blood of Jesus Christ and the perseverance of the Holy Spirit. God sent both Christ and His Spirit because He does not desire that any should perish, but that we may be saved.[60]

Jesus accomplished the great work of bridging the immeasurable gap between God and man, and the Holy Spirit now works so that we may receive and walk in the spiritual life. God has called us, Christ has made the way, and the Holy Spirit gives us life so that we can respond.

On the Day of the Lord that rift will no longer only be bridged, it will be entirely eradicated. We will never again be separated from our Holy God in spirit or in flesh. God has already declared and appointed that this is how all things *will* be and that they will never be anything other. For the hope found in this promise, made to His children as their inheritance we soldier on in any circumstance.

Because any trial we could ever suffer is by its very nature fleeting and

---

[60] 2 Peter 3:9

temporary. Meanwhile, an absolute, immovable, indestructible, and eternal promise made by the only infallibly trustworthy being in existence, has been set aside and awaits those who persevere to the end.

Towards the end of this passage, in verse eight, we find the only verse in the entire chapter which gives any mention of Hell. Honestly, I was sorely tempted when writing this book to "beef up" this subject. While much has been said of the contrast between Heaven and Hell, in sermons and theological writings, this particular passage that we are dissecting only briefly addresses the lake of fire.

Yet if we read it carefully and faithfully, this singular verse carries its own grave implications. It does not tell us much concerning the place of Hell so much as it tells us about its inhabitants. Remember who it is that is speaking in this passage. God is dictating these truths to the Apostle John. As such, it is by God's authority alone that the line is being drawn, defining who will be called children of God in the coming Kingdom, and who will pass away with the kingdom of darkness.

The distinction can be crudely summarized as, those who conquer will be counted among His children while those who remain conquered will be His enemies. Because when one is set against God, they are not actually free. They are merely under the rule and reign of a different king; one who actively wages war against the coming Kingdom of Heaven. In verse eight we see this line drawn all the more clearly as God defines those who will be counted among His enemies.

The Cowardly:

Those who are too enslaved by fear to lay hold of the glorious promise set before them, or to stand firm and wage war against the evil which has been made known to them. They do not have the courage to oppose the kingdom they are living in, and to claim God as their King and Lord.

The Faithless:

Those who have refused to believe, or to persevere in believing. They see God's glory on display, they hear the Word, they are told of the nature of God, and yet they say that there is no God. Or they fall into a delusion that the God of Scripture is not the true God, and so they fashion one of their own making. Choosing then, to believe in a god they can believe in without the need to exercise faith.

The Detestable/Vile:

Those who take pleasure in what is wicked and repulsive. They rejoice at what ought to make them weep. Pleasures are found in that which grieves the Spirit, and often they go so far as to find their identity in those things. Such people would find no joy for them in Heaven, because they have chosen to seek fulfillment and derive happiness from that which cannot exist in the age to come.

The Murderers:

Those who have placed greater value on their own wants than they have on the lives of those who have been created in the image of God. They have given a higher priority to their own hate, anger, lusts, and jealousy than they have in life which the Spirit of God has breathed into His children.

The Sexually Immoral:

Those who have elevated the temporary and unfulfilling pleasures of sexual sin over the immaculate and eternal rewards of righteous obedience. They have been overcome and conquered by their lusts, and carnal yearnings, and have decided that it is better to succumb to those base temptations than to cling to their purity, their spouse, or even to God.

The Sorcerers:

Those who seek supernatural power to bend and control towards their own ends. They have chosen not only to remain lord over their own lives, but to garner power and further enforce their corrupt will. Such a person has not subjected themselves in obedience or dependency to the Lord Most High. He is not their King in this world, how will He be their Father in the next?

The Idolaters:

Those who have devoted themselves to gods of their own design and worship the creation rather than the Creator. Because in reality, submission to idols is no submission at all. We are at liberty to maintain our own autonomy and self-rule when interacting with our false gods.

All Liars:

Those who are sons and daughters of Satan, the father of lies. This includes lies to others, lies to ourselves, and lies to God. While God cannot be deceived by our dishonesty, we can by lying to Him deceive ourselves. We must decide that the truth is of immeasurably greater importance than our comfort, our plans, our desires, and even our very lives.

Note that God's definition of a citizen of the kingdom of darkness and slave to the old world, stretches past the outward actions and reaches the heart. It is in the depths of our hearts that we find either the fire of true regeneration by the indwelling Spirit, or the lurking darkness of our unrepentant sin.

This passage does not say that those who become afraid, those who doubt and question and wrestle, those who commit heinous acts, those who have killed, those who have faltered in their purity, those who have prayed wrongly, those who have a flawed view of God, or those who have lied.

Someone can lie in weakness without being a liar or in a moment of inspiration tell the truth without being an honest person. Similar to how someone can perform CPR and not be a doctor or fail to score a touchdown without ceasing to be a football player.

The repentant and restored Christian, who is daily being sanctified by the Spirit, may at times fall into a number of sins which have been listed here and still be genuinely saved. Likewise, someone who professes Christ and even seems to flawlessly represent Him in their outward actions may actually be motivated by any of these sins of the heart. Ultimately their good works will be worth nothing. They will be as filthy rags, because good works are not how we earn salvation, they are how we walk it out.

All good works which are motivated by cowardice, faithlessness, perversion, hatred, lust, pride, idolatry, or deceit are nothing more than jewelry and makeup on a corpse. They possess all the trappings of life without any of the substance. The difference is found in one party being at war with the flesh, which causes them to sin, while the other is in league with it.

While the child of God looks at their salvation brought to them by God and is prompted to reply in worshipful obedience to Him, the professing Christian, or "spiritual" or "good" person has typically made an idol out of their preferred afterlife. Because living "rightly" is a means to reach their Heaven. Their mock righteousness is meant to acquire comfort in this life, the next, or both.

Ultimately, this will leave them spiritually dead yet convinced of their own vitality, or it will drive them ever further into their sin once they discover that the economy of Heaven does not work that way. The earned reward of those who cling to what kills them, and reject God's extended hand, is the lake of fire. The reward of God's people is that which has been secured by the blood of Jesus Christ. Eternity with the Great I Am! The New Jerusalem, the New Heaven, the New Earth, life evermore with death banished forever.

Sinful pleasures of this life will not be thought of fondly in the pains of the second death, and even the most soul-wrenching suffering of this life will be turned into praises in eternal life. God has promised us an inheritance worthy of every second of warfare.

If you read these words and find that you have not submitted to the Lord, that you do not love Him, that you are not His child and He is not your God, know that He is not a cruel deity who earnestly seeks out any opportunity He can to punish you and send you to Hell. Rather, God's desire to rescue you is such that He has made a clear and entirely sufficient path through what was once an impassable and insurmountable obstacle. Jesus Christ has died for sins to be forgiven, He has gone into Hell and borne the torment for all who would cry out to Him, He has fulfilled the debt that has been earned by the wicked and the wayward.

By His resurrection we know that His sacrifice was sufficient, and that the everlasting hope which we can claim has been secured. Over the course of three days He bore an eternity's worth of torment for every soul which would repent, turn, and be saved. Receive this inheritance and be made alive by the same Spirit who raised Jesus from the dead!

By His strength, hold fast, because Jesus waits as the living anchor of our hope at the right hand of the Father. He intercedes for you day and night before our God. He waits eagerly for the day when He will fly to our final rescue. If this is not yet your inheritance, it can be! The Holy Spirit can breathe new life into you at this very moment. Though you are being born again into a war, you are also born into a beautiful promise. A promise of freedom!

Will you die to death, forsake the kingdom of this world, and be raised into eternal life? His most wonderful promise is yours for the taking. One which He has offered not out of obligation but out of a desire that His children may be rescued. Do not let another moment pass you by without laying hold of the treasure of Heaven.

To the Christian, walk in courageous faith, trusting that the God who has been faithful in everything will be faithful to you in this. Hope always and remain steadfast. He will give you the strength to persevere, and in the end it will all be worth it.

Chapter 10

Turning our Eyes: How do we persevere in hope?

Forced perspective typically refers to making something that is small appear larger or smaller than it truly is. This strategy was employed to perfection in the Lord of The Ring trilogy where the director and production team were able to have two regular sized humans appear to be drastically different in size even while occupying the same set. The feat is accomplished by staging the subjects in such a way that the established point of view will give the *illusion* that what is small is actually large or vice versa.

Another example which can be accomplished easily while you read this book is to hold your thumb up on one hand, close one eye, and move the thumb closer to your eyes until it blocks out this entire page from your vision. We both know that your thumb is not really larger than this page, but if you were to spend every day with your thumb occupying that space in your field of vision you may eventually begin to believe that it may just actually be that big.

Our hearts can function in much the same way as our eyes. Even in Scripture we find cries to God for Him to "open the eyes of our heart".[61] What we center our attention on, and what we saturate our heart with will loom over our minds and cast its shadow or its light over our every

---

[61] Ephesian 1:18

thought.

How can we expect to have hope when our vision is entirely consumed by what would strike fear into our hearts, and cause us to despair? In the same way that holding your thumb up to your eye will make it seem larger than a book, holding the woes and worry and strife of the world ever before your eyes will eventually cause that to be all that you see. It will all seem so much larger than you, larger even than God.

Think, in a generation which seems so beset by depression and angst, what is held before our faces all day long? We live in an information age where all of the world's troubles are not only available but are foisted upon us by innumerable outlets. There is this general feeling that you are responsible for each and every tragedy or injustice that enters your realm of knowledge and that if you remain quiet or undisturbed then you are unfeeling and cruel. Not only this, but we are attached by the palm to this fountain of ever-increasing woe, and our vision is almost constantly fixed upon it. We view our world through phones and computers and televisions, and it does shape our perception of reality and of truth.

How can we persevere in hope if we put ourselves at such a severe disadvantage? Why do we handicap ourselves in our pursuit of peace? Am I saying, as some do, that we should fully do away with our phones and our televisions? I am certainly not. There was a time when I was convinced of this tactic, and for some it may still be necessary as Christ commanded those who followed Him to be willing to cast their hand and their eye into the fire if they caused them to sin.[62]

We have access to edifying material on both, and there is no doubt that there are many uses for the smartphone for the Kingdom of God. However, we must acknowledge that there is a constant war for our attention, both in the natural world as well as in the supernatural. If we enter the battlefield of our phones and televisions without that in mind, then we are likely to be led by the nose down the pathway of despair and hopelessness.

How do we combat this? How do we set ourselves up for success to persevere in hope until the end, and even to be an ally to our despairing brothers and sisters in Christ when they feel they cannot carry on? As the hymn says, we must turn our eyes upon Jesus, and the things of earth will grow strangely dim in the light of His mercy and grace.

This holds true in Scripture. We must turn our eyes upon Jesus, and by His Holy Spirit be uplifted and refreshed. There are a few passages which I will reference in this chapter, but the primary one is listed below.

"No one has ascended into heaven except he who descended from heaven, the Son of Man. And as Moses lifted up the serpent in the wilderness, so

---

[62] Matthew 18:18-19

must the Son of Man be lifted up, that whoever believes in him may have

eternal life. "For God so loved the world, that he gave his only Son, that

whoever believes in him should not perish but have eternal life. For God

did not send his Son into the world to condemn the world, but in order that

the world might be saved through him."

John 3:13-17 (ESV)

There are a few key points of interest that I want to address within this particular passage. Firstly, let us bring our attention to the repetition of Christ's purpose in coming to Earth. Secondly, the significance of Christ comparing Himself to the brazen serpent in the wilderness. Thirdly, the position we must hold Christ in within our hearts in order to benefit from His majesty.

Our first point is the fundamental truth of the Gospel. Namely, that Christ came to save sinners. This was His chief purpose, and was the reason that He descended, the reason He was given, and the reason that He was sent. Three times in this passage alone we see it reiterated that Christ came to save us unto eternal life. Christ *descended* so that we could look upon His life and His sacrifice and be saved.

He was *given* by His Father out of God's love so that we could be saved. God *sent* Him to us so that we could have eternal life. There are countless hours that we could spend hammering away on this alone. Be assured that it is not by accident that God is so thorough in communicating this point and in settling it in our brains as the absolute truth on which everything else hinges.

What purpose does this focus on Christ's mission ultimately serve in helping us to persevere in hope? As Paul says, if Christ did not raise from the dead, we are most of all to be pitied.[63] If Christ was not given to us for our salvation, then there is nothing in this world that can offer hope that withstands the coming judgment and the present suffering.

Additionally, I think the fact that Christ uses three different causes for His sacrifice is neither insignificant nor contradictory. We may at first think that Christ bouncing between these three terms betrays an inconsistency. In actuality, He is being gracious to us by removing routes by which the enemy would try to cause us to doubt.

Christ descended, freely and by His own divine will He stepped down to Earth. This tells us that He is fully capable as the Divine Being, and that He has chosen the work which He has undertaken.

Christ was given, as the sacrificial lamb, perfect and spotless. He is the greatest gift, the Son of Promise where God has shown us that He will go as far and further for our rescue than He even asked Abraham to go.[64]

---

[63] 1 Corinthians 15:17
[64] Genesis 22

Christ was sent, as the first missionary Christ was sent with purpose and a divine appointment where our entire salvation rests on His ability to fulfill.

In this teaching by Jesus, we are bolstered against the lies of the enemy when he works to damage our faith in the sufficient work of Christ. Satan cannot tell me that Christ is unfit for the task, for He alone has descended from Heaven. That serpent cannot tell me that Christ saves me out of obligation and with resentment for Christ chose the work. I know that God saves me out of His great love because He gave to me His Great Gift.

I know that Satan cannot outwit or circumvent the salvation offered to me and the eternal life secured for me, because it was a military mission of conquest which was conceived by the Father, executed by the Son, and is now held fast by the Spirit. He cannot be outwitted by that outcast who lurks now in the shadows until his day of final judgment.

Jesus hearkens back to a story from Numbers in order to drive home the significance of His loving errand, prescribing the manner of our rescue and our perseverance.

"From Mount Hor they set out by the way to the Red Sea, to go around the land of Edom. And the people became impatient on the way. And the people spoke against God and against Moses, "Why have you brought us up out of Egypt to die in the wilderness? For there is no food and no water, and we

loathe this worthless food." Then the Lord sent fiery serpents among the people, and they bit the people, so that many people of Israel died. And the people came to Moses and said, "We have sinned, for we have spoken against the Lord and against you. Pray to the Lord, that he take away the serpents from us." So Moses prayed for the people. And the Lord said to Moses, "Make a fiery serpent and set it on a pole, and everyone who is bitten, when he sees it, shall live." So Moses made a bronze serpent and set it on a pole. And if a serpent bit anyone, he would look at the bronze serpent and live."

Numbers 21:4-9 (ESV)

This passage is rich with Gospel imagery, and with the gift of viewing all of the Old Testament through the lens of the cross we can quickly identify several reasons why Christ referenced this story.

Firstly, the people grumble against the Lord. He has lovingly answered their prayers and led them out of their slavery in Egypt, and continued to miraculously provide for them while they wander through the wilderness. It was their own cowardice and sinful doubt which led them to wander for forty years, and yet God in His faithful love and kindness did not abandon them to fend for themselves. Out of His generosity He provided for their needs, and still out of the overflow of their hearts they cursed His love.

Similarly, the unregenerate man curses God and grumbles against Him because he feels that God has dealt unfairly with him. Even though God brings the rain on the righteous and the unrighteous alike and His common grace provides for the needs of even the most wretched rebel.[65] Often the regenerate believer, when rescued out of their bondage to sin, may still find themselves grumbling against their liberator when they are tasked with walking through the barren places on the road to glory.

Secondly, we find the messianic imagery in the deadly snake bites, that is the affliction which identifies the need of the people for rescue. There is a two-fold imagery here that applies first to the unbeliever and second to the believer.

In the imagery for the unbeliever, death as the just wages of sin afflicts the people. In their rebellion against the Lord and their kicking against His love, believing in no small part that they would be better stewards of their own fate, they find themselves beset by vipers which cause death to enter the camp. We see that the people cry out to God to remove this affliction which their own wickedness has brought about, but instead He raises up a symbol of His saving grace extended towards them.

They must look up for their salvation and have faith that God is good and just and will faithfully honor His promises. For the unbeliever, this is their eternal salvation. They look upon the bronze serpent of Christ lifted up on

---

[65] Matthew 5:45

the cross and though they are bitten by their sin they will not suffer the eternal death which justly follows.

To the believer, this imagery relates not only to how they have come to faith, but how they persevere in it. Though we have been rescued from our bondage we may grumble against the Lord as we still have to trudge through the suffering and trials of this world before reaching the Promised Land.

We often find ourselves snake-bitten by the many troubles that afflict us in our time here and will likely be tempted to succumb to their effects. While we are already spared our eternal death and this can never be undone, still we are abused by many struggles. So, we look at the bronze serpent and we live.

In our distress we must look to Christ and be reminded that not only has He endured every suffering and been tried in every way as we have, enduring betrayal, poverty, injustice, beatings, death, and even Hell itself, but He has gone so far as to overcome all suffering and blaze a path for us to the Throne of God.

Finally, there is importance placed on the nature of the serpent being bronze. Not only is the serpent already the opposite image of the serpent in the garden by whom all humanity was deceived and condemned, not only does this strike a parallel with the old Adam introducing sin and death through his rebellion while the New Adam brings saving life, but even the bronze used is symbolic in Scripture of the cleansing of sins.[66]

When Solomon constructed the Temple in Jerusalem, the Holy of Holies was wrought in gold to signify the glory of God.[67] Yet for the high priest to enter the Holy of Holies he first had to conduct the atoning sacrifice at the bronze altar where the stain of his sin would be washed away, and he would be able to stand righteously before the Lord and not die.[68] Again, this is the majestic work of Christ that in our hopeless state we may look to Him and live.

Our great danger, once we have received these divine promises, is to place them on the shelf and never look at them again. God's Holy Spirit breathes life into us and ignites the fire in our souls, and too often those who find themselves struggling against despair will find that the fire has been neglected for some time. If the promise and work of Christ is not held in front of your eyes always, if He is not lifted up in your sight and kept before everything else, then you will quickly find yourself overwhelmed by everything that fights to arrest your attention and trample you underfoot.

For us to benefit daily from Christ's hope-sustaining life He must be raised up in our hearts.

---

[66] Romans 5:12-19
[67] 1 Kings 6
[68] 2 Chronicles 4:1-22

Returning to the idea of forced perspective, consider if you were to stand five miles outside your city with a 1:100 scale model of the largest building directly in front of you. From that distance and from that perspective, the scale model would *appear* to be larger than the building off in the distance. I live not far from Atlanta where the tallest building is over 930 feet tall. Even a 1:100 scale model would be nearly ten feet tall, towering over me by almost four feet.

It would be larger than me, heavier than me, and sturdier than me. I wouldn't be able to carry it or even move it very far at all with every bit of my strength. If left to my own understanding, I might even begin to think that this towering structure in front of me would certainly outclass the smaller figure so far out of reach. However, when that model is placed side by side with the original, the model would not even reach the second of the building's fifty-five floors. In terms of architecture, strength, or weight it would not even be worth mentioning in the same breath.

If we do not lift Christ up, we condemn ourselves to a desperate struggle against an enemy whose might is not worth mentioning in the same breath as that of our Savior. The more our vision becomes filled with the things of this world, the weaker our grip will become on our everlasting hope, and the dimmer the flame of the Spirit will burn in our eyes. But when Christ is lifted up so that all may look to Him, and we are day by day and moment by moment reminded of His majesty and power, His glory will shine a light on the things of darkness and expose them as the frail and impotent creatures they are.

Imagine holding a blade of grass side by side with the sun, burning in all its fury, and you would never expect it to be able to survive for even a moment before being utterly consumed. This is the type of disparity available to us when we cling to our hope in Christ. To do so He must be high and lifted up in our hearts, enthroned on our praises and viewed in His glory. Do not rely on your own strength to endure. God does not do all the work in saving us just to leave us to our own devices to persevere.

By intentional fellowship with the Holy Spirit, Spirit led study of the Word, and Spirit empowered prayer before the mercy seat, keep Christ constantly before the eyes of your heart. This is how you persevere in Hope. Because when we turn our eyes upon Jesus all the things of Earth grow strangely dim in the light of His glory and grace.

www.ingramcontent.com/pod-product-compliance
Lightning Source LLC
Chambersburg PA
CBHW011237120626
46549CB00009B/3299